WORKHORSE
PROPS

G000232165

WORKHORSE PROPS

PROP AIRCRAFT AROUND THE WORLD

IL 18

GERRY MANNING

Airlife
England

FRONT COVER:
A Vintage Airlines Dakota at Kissimmee, Florida base, before its next flight to Key West.

BACK COVER:
TOP LEFT:
Privateer Tanker number 30 running all four Wright R2600 engines as it parks at Chico, CA.
TOP RIGHT:
The only prupose-built water bomber is the Canadian CL-215. Operated by the Province of Ontario, C-GBXQ Tanker number 261 is at Dryden.
BOTTOM:
Green Airways Otter C-FMEL lands on Red Lake amid a cloud of spray.

PAGE 1:
Grumman Ag Cat crop sprayer N56426.

PAGE 2:
This Ilyushin Il-18 was used by East Germany's airline Interflug. With reunification it moved to Berline, a Berlin-based charter operator.

Copyright © 1995 by Gerry Manning

First published in the UK in 1995 by Airlife Publishing Ltd

British Library Cataloguing in Publication Data
A catalogue record for this book is available from the British Library

ISBN 1 85310 490 6

All rights reserved. No part of this book may be reproduced or transmitted in any form or by any means, electronic or mechanical including photocopying, recording or by any information storage and retrieval system, without permission from the Publisher in writing.

Printed in Hong Kong.

Airlife Publishing Ltd

101 Longden Road, Shrewsbury SY3 9EB, England

INTRODUCTION

The next time you get into a jet airliner to travel, be it for business or pleasure, take the trouble to look out of the window as you taxi out to take-off or taxi in after landing. For you may well see on the unfashionable far side of the airport, well away from the smart new terminal buildings, aircraft types that you recognise, and think to yourself, 'But surely no one is still flying those. Aren't they all in museums?'

The answer is 'yes', someone is still flying them, and 'no', they are not yet all in museums. They are the 'workhorse props' and without them the rich tapestry of air transport would be the poorer. Without them many parts of the world would simply not have an air service.

These 'workhorses' carry cargo, fight fires, operate in the bush from fields and lakes, take tourists to remote sites in the world, and perform many more tasks. Long may they continue.

Gerry Manning
Liverpool
December 1995

AUTHOR'S NOTE

If you have found the world of 'workhorse props' interesting and would like to keep up to date with them, then *Propliner Magazine* is recommended. Published quarterly by subscription, from 'New Roots', Sutton Green Road, Sutton Green, Guildford, Surrey GU4 7QD, England.

ACKNOWLEDGEMENTS

The author wishes to thank the following people: John Downey for the original partnership; Steve McDonald for advice and for first planting the idea of doing a book solo; Dave Parry for some of the travel arrangements; and George Pick of George Pick Airtours for the rest of the travel bookings and most of the flights in old aircraft.

C-FERM's nose art.

ABOVE:
De Havilland Canada DHC3 Otter C-GYYS of Northwest Flying sits at Nestor Falls Sea Plane Base (SPB), cargo door open awaiting its next load.

RIGHT:
Its Pratt & Whitney R1340 engine turning, DHC3 Otter C-GMDG of Northern Wilderness Outfitters taxis into its dock on Rainy Lake.

BUSH FLYING

A look at a map of Canada will reveal the sheer size of the country, some 38.5 million square miles to the United States of America's 36 million. In this area Canada has a population of just 26.5 million people; by comparison the USA has 249 million. A further look at the map of Canada will reveal that most of the largest cities such as Toronto, Montreal and Vancouver are in the south of the country near the US border. This means that the vast part of Canada is largely empty of people. With few people there are few towns, few towns mean few roads to connect them. The result of this is only one means of transport for the people who live and work in the Canadian bush: the aeroplane. Not just any aeroplane will do, as it will have to land without long runways, have to use lakes to land where there is no other long flat surface, and have to operate in a very bleak and harsh winter environment where the lakes are frozen and snow covers the land. It is no small wonder that the Canadian aviation industry has produced a range of aircraft well able to operate in anything that nature can throw up against them.

The ultimate 'bush' aircraft has to be the de Havilland Canada DHC2 Beaver. After the Second World War the designers of de Havilland Canada set to work on a bush aircraft to meet the needs of the Canadian outback. Before going ahead with the design they talked to the potential users of the type to find out what specific features they would need for their own operations. One such operation was the Ontario Provincial Air Service (OPAS), the provincial government's air unit. They suggested a number of specific needs, such as having doors able to take a fuel drum. The design originally equipped the aircraft with a 330hp Gipsy Queen engine, but when the 450hp Pratt & Whitney Wasp Junior radial air-cooled piston engine was available this was substituted and was found to give an excellent STOL (Short Take-Off and Landing) performance.

The Beaver was first flown from Downsview, Ontario on 16 August 1947 fitted with a wheeled undercarriage. In addition to the pilot there was accommodation for up to six passengers or freight. With normal fuel load and reserves the Beaver could carry 1,350lb of cargo for 470 miles and take off using a 595-foot length of strip in still air conditions. During the long winter months in Canada the Beaver could operate on skis. For operations in backwoods areas where there were insufficient flat strips the many lakes could be utilised by the fitting of floats. During the late 1950s one Beaver was fitted with a very large pair of wheels with very low pressure tyres at only 7 psi (pounds per square inch). This was to enable the aircraft to operate in the far arctic north of Canada off totally unprepared strips of ground. The idea worked very well and was used by a number of aircraft.

The first type development of the aeroplane was the Beaver II, a re-engined airframe with the British Alvis Leonides 550hp radial piston engine fitted together with a three-blade propeller. This version was not put into production despite working well enough.

In the early 1960s people started to look at putting a turbo engine into the Beaver. Most of these ad hoc conversions were discontinued when de Havilland Canada announced the Beaver III powered by a Pratt & Whitney Canada PT6 of 550 shaft horsepower. This turbo engine was much lighter in weight than the Wasp Junior and so the designers were able to extend the fuselage by five feet to taken an extra fuel tank and two extra passengers. The Beaver III flew for the first time on New Year's Eve, 31 December 1963. The production run for the Turbo Beaver III was sixty aircraft, the bulk going to OPAS and other government bodies.

The biggest users of the Beaver were the US Army and US Air Force who between them operated nearly 1,000 aircraft. As these were declared surplus they were snapped up by small backwoods operators who found the cost of operating a surplus military piston-powered aircraft far cheaper than the operation of the expensive engined PT6 Turbo Beavers. The Beaver has proved to be the right aircraft for the job, and with no sign of a suitable replacement at a price the backwoods operators can afford the Beaver will be found flying long into the next century.

So successful was the Beaver in service with OPAS that they soon asked de Havilland Canada to produce a similar aircraft to the Beaver but with twice its capacity. A promise to order over twenty of the new aircraft was sufficient incentive for work to start on the new design. The first name considered was the King Beaver, but this soon changed to the DHC3 Otter. Basically the Otter is the Beaver's big brother and follows the same basic layout. Fitted to the aircraft as standard is a double freight door and the cabin can carry up to nine passengers with a crew of two. The seats for the passengers were able to be folded away to the side of the cabin when freight was carried.

The prototype Otter first flew from Downsview, Ontario on 12 December 1951 and was fitted with a 600hp Pratt & Whitney Wasp R1340 air-cooled radial engine. As with the Beaver, the Otter found favour with the US Army who operated over 150 aircraft. Many of these have returned to Canada for use in the backwoods. Operations mirror those of the Beaver with the use of wheels, skis and floats. The low pressure tyres mentioned earlier were used on Otters also.

De Havilland Canada did not themselves make a turbo Otter, but one private engineering company fitted one with a Pratt & Whitney Canada PT6 of 662shp and first flew this in the latter part of 1978. The Turbo Otter is a very rare aircraft today whilst the piston-powered one soldiers on as a workhorse, again with no sign of a replacement design.

Another seemingly irreplaceable aircraft operated in Canada's backwoods is the Noorduyn Norseman, pre-dating the DHC2 Beaver by over a decade. Work was started on the design of the Norseman late in 1934 by Bob Noorduyn. He approached various potential operators and their pilots for their views on what features the new design should have. The new aircraft emerged as a conventional design with a high wing, single engine and a wide cabin featuring a loading door able to take rolled-in fuel drums. Besides the single pilot there was room for up to nine passengers or a mix of cargo and people.

The prototype Norseman took to the air for the first time on 14 November 1935. It was flown first as a float plane, the first flight taking place off the St Lawrence river in Montreal, and power for this was provided by a single Wright Whirlwind radial air-cooled piston engine of 420hp.

Production went ahead with the Norseman II, this being almost identical to the Mark I except for a slight increase in weight. Only three were produced as the Wright Whirlwind was not powerful enough. The Norseman III was re-engined with a Pratt & Whitney Wasp of 420 hp. This again was underpowered and just three aircraft were built. For the Norseman IV a Pratt & Whitney R1340 Wasp of 550hp was fitted. This boost in power was to prove decisive as all subsequent Norseman variants were fitted with this engine. The Mark IV first flew in November 1936, so it had taken a year from the first flight of the Mark I to reach the definitive aircraft.

The Norseman entered service with the Royal Canadian Air Force and then later with the US Army Air Force. The USAAF operated approximately 750 aircraft with the designation C-64. The weight of this was increased, as was the fuel tankage, to become the Norseman Mark VI. It was the designers' wish to save the Mark V as the 'V' for victory aircraft based upon Prime Minister Winston Churchill's famous 'V' sign. The first Mark Vs were delivered to OPAS in June 1945 and were basically civilianised versions of the Mark VI. Production of the Norseman continued until 1959 when the last aircraft of just over 900 flew on 17 December of that year, a remarkable production run of twenty-four years from the first flight of the prototype Norseman Mark I.

To this day Norsemans can be found in Canada operating on wheels, skis and floats depending upon the season or the location, and as with many bush aircraft there is no obvious design to replace them at a reasonable price.

As a footnote to the Norseman, one USAAF C-64 was involved in an incident that even today has never been fully cleared up. It occurred on 15 December 1944 when the famous band leader Glen Miller, who was then a Major in the US Army and the director of its band, boarded a Norseman for a flight to Paris. The aircraft disappeared and no trace of it or the occupants has ever been bound. The speculations as to what happened have ranged between the totally bizarre and the simply unbelievable. The favourite explanation seems to be that the aircraft was hit by bombs being jettisoned from a higher flying bomber, thus causing its destruction. The truth will probably never be known, but that is good news for the sensationalists who would not like a logical answer to the mystery.

Not every aircraft designed in Canada for use in the bush has been an instant success. One such type is from the Found Aircraft Company. This company was set up near the end of the war by two brothers, Bud and Mickey Found, who were both pilots for Trans-Canada Airlines. The design they had in mind was a small utility type, smaller than aircraft like the Beaver. Their first aircraft was designated FBA-1A and was flown for the first time by Mickey Found

on 13 July 1949 at Malton, Ontario. Only about twenty hours were put in on the airframe before it was retired the following year. The concept had proved successful and the brothers wanted to put a production version into the air. This process was to take a long time due to a number of reasons. One was that the design team was only working part-time; their full-time jobs were with Avro Canada. Funding also caused the longest delays and it was not until August 1960, ten years after the FBA-1A was retired, that the first FBA-2A was flown from Malton. This aircraft was a basic high-wing monoplane with space for four people, powered by a 250hp Lycoming liquid-cooled piston engine. The prototype flew with a wheeled undercarriage, but was later flown with floats from Toronto Island airport.

The plan was to have two different production versions available to customers, the FBA-2B with a tricycle nose-wheel undercarriage and the FBA-2C with a tail-wheel undercarriage. The latter was deemed better for bush operations from rough unprepared strips, and so became the only type built. The production FBA-2C had a longer fuselage than the prototype and had room for five people. The first flight of a production aircraft took place on 9 May 1962. Regrettably this aircraft was destroyed in a crash near Brampton the following month, resulting in the death of the pilot.

A total of twenty-seven aircraft including the prototype was built, and each entered service with small charter operators across Canada. It did its job without being a brilliant success nor an abject failure. A few Founds can still be seen operating today. If the design had one small problem it was the lack of a wing support strut. It was not that the wing needed the extra support, but when the aircraft is operated on floats, as so many bush aircraft are, then the wing strut is used to grab hold of and manhandle the aircraft around the dock. Found Brothers Aviation closed down at the end of 1968 due to lack of orders for aircraft and a cashflow problem.

Most aircraft designs flying in the bush are single-engine types. One exception to this is the Beech 18. This aircraft is one of the most common designs to be found in the remote places. Powered by two Pratt & Whitney R985 nine-cylinder air-cooled radial piston engines, the Beech 18 was first flown in January 1937 from the flat lands of Wichita, Kansas. The type was used during the Second World War for basic twin training and as a navigation and bomb-aiming trainer, with some five thousand airframes being built.

The Beech 18 has accommodation for five to seven passengers and a crew of two. The aircraft can be found on wheels, skis and floats. The floatplane version is quite distinctive as it has a large ventral fin to offset the extra side area of the EDO floats. As well as operations in the bush on floats, many Beech 18s can be found at large airports employed on night cargo operations feeding small parcels to hub centres.

The only other twin-engined type to be found in any numbers in the bush is the de Havilland DHC6 Twin Otter. It was a logical development for the manufacturer at last to design an aircraft both to supplement and replace the very successful DHC3 Otter. It was planned that the new aircraft would have two engines, for several reasons: one, it would improve performance, both in speed and lift capacity; two, it would obviously be safer to operate; three, it would have a high passenger appeal; and four, it would be able to pick up orders in the commuter market, an area the Otter has not sold into.

The new aircraft had to have a short take-off and landing (STOL) performance; to work on the Twin Otter's design and to use as many common parts with the DHC3 Otter as possible. The engine choice had to be a turboprop for running costs and reliability. This resulted in the fitting of two Pratt & Whitney (Canada) PT6A turboprops of 620 shaft horsepower each. On 20 May 1965 the new Twin Otter took to the air for the first time. The sales were in the early days from commuter airlines as the aircraft was expensive to buy for some of the small bush operators. Not having such worries about the cost of new expensive designs OPAS, which forms part of the Ministry of Natural Resources and has been such a leading force in the development and operation of Canadian designs in bush operations, was among the lead customers operating the fourth built aircraft.

Twin Otters can be found like all good workhorses operating on wheels; these include the oversize low pressure tyres, skis and floats. Most of the OPAS aircraft operate in this latter mode. One commuter airline, Air BC of Richmond, Vancouver Island, British Columbia, uses its Twin Otters in a mix of float and wheeled undercarriages to ferry up to eighteen passengers at a time around the province.

One of the main industries in the bush or backwoods is tourism. These tourists do not want the high-rise hotel and swimming pool, the beach across the road and a nightclub disco booming out a high decibel level of noise until the early hours of the morning. What they want is to see nature and visit a totally unspoilt part of the world. Fishing and

hunting are the favourite pastimes, and a complex infrastructure has been built up to satisfy the needs, using aeroplanes. Among the companies who run these trips is Kashabowie Outposts Ltd, operating a single DHC2 Beaver from Shebandowan Lake, some sixty-five miles west of Thunder Bay, one of the main towns in Ontario's Sunset Country. These places are very accessible from the United States as they are within a day's drive of such major population centres as Chicago and the twin cities of Minneapolis/St Paul.

When the tourists arrive at the operator's base they are flown in the Beaver to one of a number of outpost cabins that can accommodate between two and twelve people in what is described as rustic comfort. The cabins are usually fitted out with propane stoves to cook with and refrigerators to keep fresh any fish that are caught. These locations are very remote and have no roads to them nor landing strips and so the Beaver will operate on floats and drop the fishermen at the cabin door. In the lakes of the area can be found a wide variety of fish such as wall-eye, lake trout, small mouth bass, muskie and northern pike. To get out on the lake to fish, motorboats will be provided. Many of the fish will be in excess of 20lb in weight and may have been caught previously as a policy of returning the larger fish to the water is encouraged.

For those who want to hunt, ever more remote locations are available, some of which are tented camps. The game hunted will usually be the moose or black bear. Strict rules for the acquisition of a Canadian Hunting Licence apply, and the would-be hunter must be able to prove prior experience in this field. Kashabowie Outposts offers trips lasting from three to seven days at a total of eleven locations.

On a far larger scale than Kashabowie is Rusty Myers Flying Service Ltd of Fort Frances, Ontario. They have provided a flying service to north-west Ontario for nearly

Beech 18 CF-TBH engineless at Sioux Lookout awaiting the scrapman.

fifty years and currently have a fleet of five twin-engined Beech 18s, two DHC2 Beavers and a single Cessna 185 Sky Wagon. All of these operate on floats from the Fort Frances sea-plane base. Fort Frances is a border town with the US state of Minnesota. The 'Fort', as it is known, is the largest town in the Rainy River area with a population of 8,000 people, pulp and paper being the chief industry. Operations are conducted so that the fisherman can leave a US city such as Milwaukee in the morning and be out at a fishing lodge later the same day.

The camps served by Rusty Myers are in two groups with nine camps located between 165 and 240 miles from base and a second batch of five camps fifty-five and sixty-five miles from base. As part of a holiday, the actual flight from base to the fishing or hunting lodge gives a panoramic view over an area of outstanding natural beauty comprising lakes and woods over a vast flat landscape. As the airline claims, they are your route to the unreachable.

At Sioux Lookout, Ontario can be found the charter company of Knobby's, also known as Sioux Air, operating a mixed fleet of DHC2 Beavers and DHC3 Otters on floats. This is a family-run business founded by Glen Clark, better known as Knobby, in 1966 after he left the Royal Canadian Air Force. Helping to run the operation is his wife Bobbie and their two daughters Kim and Donna who fly the aeroplanes. Like a number of companies they fly fishermen to remote lakeside lodges, in their case thirteen cabins on seven fish-filled lakes. Not all the cabins are for people who have to rough it. They have on offer some cabins and locations with showers, flush toilets and a camp sauna as well as a resident caretaker who will look after the site and supply ice to freeze fish catches and keep the fuel levels in the boats up. For a holiday destination that can truly be said to 'get away from it all', a flying and fishing trip must be high on any list.

Flying in the backwoods for most operators means using float-equipped aeroplanes. One operator that has carved a market in northern Ontario and only uses landplanes is Bearskin Airlines. They, like Sioux Air, are based at Sioux Lookout, but instead of operating from the lake waterfront of the town they operate from the local airport. As well as charter flights, their main operations are scheduled services connecting over twenty-six towns and cities from as far west as Winnipeg in Manitoba, to an international service across the United States border at Minneapolis, in between these calling at such wonderfully named places as Pickle Lake, Big Trout Lake and Thunder Bay. To operate all these services a fleet of twenty-seven aircraft of seven main types is used. Not for them the old Beavers, Norsemans or Otters but a largely turbine-powered fleet of aircraft such as the nineteen-seat Fairchild (Swearingen) Metro, the eighteen-seat DHC6 Twin Otter, ten-seat Beech King Airs, fourteen-seat Beech 99 Airliners, and nine-seat Piper T1040 turbo Navajos together with a number of Piper Aztecs and Cessnas.

The company was founded thirty years ago in 1963 as an air taxi service at Bearskin Lake and has grown considerably during this time and now employs over two hundred people. The scheduled services fly over 90,000 passengers per year with each month over two hundred charters being flown. Two of the charters stand out as being among the oddest the company has ever flown. The first was the carriage of 3,000lb of Colonel Sanders Kentucky Fried Chicken from Thunder Bay up to Fort Hope. The second was to transport 15,000 baby chicks from Toronto to Nicaragua in Central America, the longest charter they have ever flown.

To the west of Ontario is the province of Manitoba, and at the largest city, Winnipeg, can be found one of the larger operators of charters and schedules to the backwoods, Air

RIGHT:
Walsten Air Services Beech 18 C-FCUK at Kenora SPB.

OPPOSITE:
C-FERM Beech 18 of Rusty Myers Flying Service Ltd over the Fort Francis area. Note the large ventral fin: this is to offset the extra side area of the EDO floats.

Manitoba. It operates a fleet of four Douglas Dakotas, one as a freighter and three as passenger carriers, five Avro (Hawker Siddeley) 748s in forty-six-seat configuration, and four Curtiss C-46 Commandos as freighters. The airline flies to locations in northern Manitoba and western Ontario on both schedule and charter flights. The cargo carried by the Curtiss Commando can be up to 16,000lb in weight, and if it will fit through the door, be it a four-wheel-drive vehicle, an oil-drilling rig, or delicate computer parts, the company will carry it to where the customer wants it to go providing that there is a long enough landing strip. The company have a contract with the Hudsons Bay Company, one of the oldest trading companies in Canada, to service the reservations of northern Manitoba. Living in these are the

American Indians, or Native Americans as they are now usually known. The regular flights to the reservations carry all the goods needed for a community to function, and the aircraft is loaded up to be a flying hardware store, a grocer's, a drugstore, and every other type of store that you can think of.

For operators like Air Manitoba, the term 'air service' takes on a whole new meaning, for they provide the means for the scattered communities to stay in touch with one another, to supply goods, to travel to the big cities, and to bring in people to visit some of the most remote and yet beautiful places in Canada without spoiling the fragile environment of the area.

ABOVE:
With a cover on its Pratt & Whitney R1340 engine, Norseman VI C-FKAO of Gawleys waits for the next fishing charter on Lac Seul.

RIGHT:
Using the standard 'one float at a time' take-off procedure, Norseman VI C-FJEC of Sabourine Lake Airways lifts off from home base.

Kelner Airways HS748 C-GLTC gets its cargo loaded at home base. Pickle Lake.

C-GMAA HS748 of Air Creebec has had its pressurisation system removed to extend airframe life in its cargo role. Seen here at Pickle Lake.

BELOW:
Cessna Caravan C-FKAL of Kelner Airways stakes its claim to be one of the new workhorses of the area. The high purchase cost may deter some users.

ABOVE:
Executive transport backwoods style. Grumman Goose C-FHUZ slips into Sproat Lake with four businessmen at the end of a meeting.

LEFT:
Head to head. Otter and Beaver show the size difference between the two types at Sioux Lookout SPB.

Lost and Found. Found FBA-2c C-FSDC of
Tudhope Airways at Lost Lake.

LEFT:
Twin Otter C-GGVX of Norontair is the standard commuter in the backwoods. Seen here at Red Lake airport.

BELOW:
One of Air Manitoba's immaculate Dakotas, C-GSCC, awaits the next job at home base of Winnipeg.

The largest of the water bombers. The mighty Martin JRM-3 *Hawaii* Mars C-FLYL on its home base of Sproat Lake, Vancouver Island.

WATER BOMBERS

One of the earliest uses of the aeroplane was to fly over an area and, by the use of bombs, rockets or bullets, set that area on fire. Things have today come full circle when an aeroplane will fly over a target and bomb it to put *out* a fire. This is the world of 'water bombing' where the target is a forest on fire and the job of the aeroplane is to put out that fire either by dropping water direct onto the flames or by dropping a retardant chemical in the path of the fire to stop it spreading to a larger area.

The forest fire is a natural phenomenon usually caused by a strike of lightning. Man, however, has often been the cause either by discarding bits of broken glass that can act as a magnifier of the sun's rays, thus causing a hotspot on tinder-dry leaves and twigs, or simply by lighting a fire for camping, which without proper care or supervision can spread very quickly. A forest fire can engulf an area running into tens of thousands of acres. These fires are often many miles from the nearest roads and so a conventional wheeled fire appliance cannot drive up to the seat of the blaze and begin to deal with it.

In the state of California approximately one fifth of the land area is covered by natural forests. A very high proportion of the trees are of the conifer variety. This type of tree has a very high resin content and will therefore burn very easily. When a forest fire is in full flow the smoke can rise as high as twenty thousand feet. The smoke stack will have a strong 'drawing' power, and even the largest aircraft can be sucked into the smoke and suffer the effects of a very turbulent, wild and bucking ride. For this reason a small spotter plane such as a Cessna 0.2 Sky Master or a Beech Baron, both types being twin-engined for extra safety, will fly on ahead of the water bomber aircraft to make a reconnaissance check of the type of terrain to be flown over, to see what level of turbulence may be expected at the altitude to be flown, and to check to see that the water bomber pilot has an escape route from the fire. This is most important as not all fires are in forests on high large flat plains. The area on fire could just as easily be the side of a hill or a mountain.

An even more difficult fire to be dealt with is one burning in a canyon. The water bomber pilot has to fly down the canyon to dump his load of water or retardant on this fire. Taking into account the lack of visibility caused by the smoke from the burning trees, the disturbed air currents from the effects of the fire cause a roller-coaster ride, and this spells danger at the very low altitude the pilot has to fly in the confined space. It would not do to crash into the side of the canyon: besides doing no good at all to the pilot's health, it would simply start another fire. The spotter aircraft will also be tasked with the job of co-ordinating the water bombers aloft with the fire chief on the ground. If a fire has been burning for some days and is likely to endanger life or property, water bombers from the surrounding bases will be brought in to deal with this blaze, and the spotter aircraft could find a whole stream of water bombers arriving at the fire. In such a situation it is of the utmost importance to get them to put the load on the right spot at the right time so as to avoid a mid-air collision.

In the early days of water application on fires it was very much an ad hoc system with regard to what aircraft dealt with what fires; in fact it was possible for the owner/pilot of an aerial tanker aircraft simply to fly into the airfield from which an operation was being run and be able to join in the firefighting effort at whatever rate was being paid at that moment in time. This system was obviously not the best in the world and so the relevant authorities began a proper system of contracts.

The largest state to use water bombers is California, and in this state the forests are managed by the California Department of Forestry (CDF). The other official federal bureaux concerned with the operation are the United States Forestry Service (USFS) and the Bureau of Land Management (BLM). Between them these three bodies will control and co-ordinate the allocation of contracts to the various bidders. The system works by the process of tenders being sent out to the operators of water bombing aircraft. These companies are: Hemet Valley Flying Services of Hemet Valley, California; Aero Union of Chico, California; Hawkins & Powers of Grey Bull, Wyoming and Firbanks, Alaska; Sis-Q Flying Services, now renamed Macavia, of Santa Rosa, California; TBM Airtankers of Tulare, California; T & G Aviation of Chandler, Arizona; Lynch Flying Tankers of Billings, Montana; Central Air Services of Tucson, Arizona and Wenatchee, Washington; and Black Hills Aviation of Alamogordo, New Mexico.

The tender will usually specify that an aircraft be supplied that can drop a set number of gallons from a particular location and for a set period of time, usually the dry season which lasts essentially from May through to the end of October. In the case of a particularly dry summer the time period of the contract may well be extended. Each of the companies bids for the contracts it wants or is able to fulfil, and consequently upon this bidding process the actual contracts are awarded. A number of companies have their corporate headquarters and maintenance facilities at airfields that are water bomber stations. This 'advantage' does not necessarily mean that they get their home base. It is not at all unusual to see at these airfields on the water bomber ramp aircraft from one company awaiting their call to arms and on the next ramp the HQ of another company with aircraft not allocated to any base parked up.

For the ease of the reader the term 'water bomber' has and will be used, but it is not water that is dropped by most land-based aircraft but a chemical retardant that is dropped in a line ahead of an approaching fire with the aim that the fire will not pass that line of defence. The first chemical retardant was sodium calcium borate. The chemical was first developed in America by the US Borax Company during 1954. It was used by mixing the chemical with water. This would produce a white heavy substance, a sticky liquid that was fire-resistant for a number of hours after dropping. The down-side of this was its unacceptable toxicity, and when large amounts were used it could sterilise the soil. It was therefore replaced in 1959 with the substance known as Benonite. To this mix was added a pink dye to act as a recognition aid to the drop pilot and the spotter co-ordinating the aerial operations. This too has been replaced by diammonium phosphate (DAP), and also in use were two other types of chemical retardant, Firetrol (ammonium sulphate) and Phos Chek (ammonium phosphate). The latter two were expressly developed to be dropped by an aeroplane.

The latest type in use is GTS, which is an update of Firetrol. The modern retardant acts both as a fire blocker and as a fertiliser to regenerate growth of trees. Even though it has not be used for a long time, borate has given its name in many people's eyes to the whole process, and they will often refer to a 'borate bomber'.

The retardant chemicals are stored in large tanks by the side of the airport ramps and can pump 600 gallons per minute into an aircraft, meaning that within five minutes an aircraft can be on its way back to a fire, slightly longer if the aviation fuel needs to be topped up. When flying over tanker country it is very easy to spot the airfields used, as the concrete is usually tinted pink and stands out among the green of the forests or plains.

The state of California boasts twenty-one bases for full operations and has another five from which retardant can be uplifted. The base is usually referred to as an 'air attack base' and is manned by CDF or USFS staff. Some bases will have a mixed unit. The average manning level is six staff: the base manager, who is the fire captain, an air attack officer, usually a forest ranger, and four firefighters. Added to this is the air crew flying the tanker aircraft, normally a pilot and a co-pilot, and the ground crews to operate the aeroplanes. Most of the air attack bases will have two aircraft on station for normal conditions. If there is large fire burning in the area then air tankers from other bases at lower risks will be brought in for a maximum effort firefight. It has been known for up to sixteen tanker aircraft to work for several weeks to cope with the tens of thousands of acres burning in a real 'mega' fire.

If a summer is wet or there are no fires in an area the crew do not fly. This for them is not good news as a high proportion of their pay is made up of actual flying time. The engines of the aircraft are run every five days to keep them in first-class order, and then every two weeks an air test is flown in which the air crew will practise their skills, culminating in a drop of several thousand gallons of water on the airfield. It is reckoned that the average amount of time flown is one hundred hours in the season, but an average is just that, an average. In a very busy dry season where the pilots are moved from base to base chasing fires, over two hundred hours can be logged.

What types of aircraft are used as air tankers? The answer is that almost any propeller-driven surplus warplane or cargoplane can and has been used at some time as an air tanker. It is an economic fact of life that new aircraft are expensive to design, build and operate, and because of this it has been usual to convert old low-value airframes for this very limited task. As it has been stated, if it is a wet year there may be no fires to put out and the aircraft sit on the ground all summer flying only for crew training. No private operator could afford to have a new and shiny aircraft with such a potentially low utilisation.

The smallest aircraft to be used as an air tanker was the Boeing PT-17 Stearman. This biplane trainer was designed pre-World War Two, first flying in 1934, and becoming the most widely used basic trainer during that conflict with well over 8,000 airframes being produced before termination of production. Powered by one 220hp Continental R-670-5 radial piston engine, the Stearman was first used by the CDF in the summer of 1956 carrying either a load of 125 gallons of water or 100 gallons of borate. A

PB4Y-2 Privateer N2872G at Santa Rosa after a refuelling stop on the way to summer base at Reading in northern California.

heavier load was needed as a matter of urgency, and later on during the same year the USFS started to operate the Grumman TBM Avenger with a 600-gallon tank. The Avenger was a surplus Navy torpedo bomber having first flown in August 1941 and entering operational service at the time of the Battle of Midway in June 1942. The type remained in service with the fleet until 1954 in a number of different roles. The powerplant used was one 1,900hp Wright R2600-20 radial piston engine. As a water bomber the type can still be found in service to this day in New Brunswick on the eastern seaboard of Canada.

Most of the American-based airframes were acquired during the 1980s for use as 'Warbirds' on the airshow circuit or to be flown for pleasure by enthusiasts. Most of these aircraft have had their tanks removed and have returned to a stock military configuration together with a wartime colour scheme. The former president of the USA, George Bush, flew TBM Avengers as a Lieutenant (jg) in the United States Navy during the Pacific campaign. This fact produced a rash of Avengers all wearing the colour scheme in which his aircraft had operated.

The year 1957 saw the arrival of one of the hot-rods of the tankers, the Grumman F7F Tigercat. This ex-Navy single-seat carrier-borne fighter was powered by two 2,100hp Pratt & Whitney R2800-34w radial piston engines. The first tankers carried an 800-gallon load, but this was later upped to 1,000 gallons. This type had lots of spare power and could get to a fire far quicker than almost any other type in service. The advantage of this was that if it got to a fire before it had got out of hand it could be nipped in the bud, so to speak. The extra speed could save having to go out and fly many follow-up sorties.

The Tigercat stayed in service until the early 1980s with TBM and Sis-Q (now Macavia), and was then withdrawn from tanker service and sold to the 'Warbird' scene where they still fly to date. Basically the aircraft had appreciated in value as a collectors' item and were now worth more to a 'Warbird' operator than they were to a water bomber contractor.

Another Navy type to be operated as a tanker was the Grumman AF-2 Guardian. Originally designed to be a carrier-borne anti-submarine search and strike aircraft it was powered by one 2,400hp Pratt & Whitney R-2800-48w radial piston engine. Only a very few were converted to the tanker role, being fitted with a 850-gallon tank. By the mid-1980s both converted and unconverted Guardians were to be found out to grass at Aero Union's base at Chico in the northern part of California. Since then they have begun to trickle out to museums, and Warbird collectors.

With a conversion of only two airframes, the North American AJ (later A2) Savage was never to be destined as a major air attack water bomber. Carrying a very useful load of 2,000 gallons under the power of two 2,400hp Pratt & Whitney R2800-44 radial piston engines together with a single 4600lb-thrust Allison J33 jet engine mounted in the tail, the Savage had a career in the Navy first as an attack bomber and then as a flight refuelling tanker. It may have been the first occasion when one tanker aircraft became a tanker of a different type. The type had a short life in civilian garb, being used only for a couple of years in the mid-1960s. Following the crash of one, the other example was withdrawn from use at Burbank. Only one Savage is still to be found to this day and that is at the US Navy museum in Pensacola, Florida.

Perhaps the most exotic of the warplanes used in the air-tanking role was the Northrop P-61 Black Widow. This design was a World War Two night fighter powered by two 2,000hp Pratt & Whitney R2800-65 radial piston engines. A later version was designated as a reconnaissance aircraft under the designation F-15A (later RF-61C) Reporter. Thirty-six were built in 1946 and from these, three were fitted with a 1,800-gallon tank in the belly during 1964. The last of the three crashed in New Mexico in 1970. This was a great pity as the type today would have fetched a very high price with museums or collectors.

Most of the other World War Two warplanes converted to the water bomber role have had far longer lives and some are still in service to this day or have only been withdrawn from use in the past few years. In this category is that most famous of United States bombers the Boeing B-17 Flying Fortress. After a long and distinguished war career the US military used the aircraft in assorted roles until as late as 1960. This was the year that the first water bomber conversions started. A total of twenty-three mainly F & G models were converted. The bomb bay was modified to hold either a 1,800- or a 2,000-gallon tank with four doors. This could be dropped in a long sequence or all at once for maximum damping effect. The sound of the Flying Fortress's four Wright R1820 1,200hp radial piston engines could be heard over the forests of America until the mid-1980s.

By that time those still flying had, like the F7F Tigercat described earlier, appreciated in value so much due to the growing popularity of the Warbird movement that they were snapped up one by one to join flying museums or as static exhibits at USAF bases as part of their heritage programme. A number of historic water bomber types have in fact been traded into the USAF museums in exchange for newer aircraft such as the Douglas C-118 (DC-6). More of that type later. Two Flying Fortresses had a new career when they finished their lives as air tankers: they starred in the 1989 film *Memphis Belle*, for which they were brought across the Atlantic ocean to Duxford aerodrome in Cambridge for this epic about the wartime 8th Air Force.

Still in service to this date are the two most famous of light bombers used by the United States Army Air Force in World War Two. These are the North American B-25 Mitchell and the Douglas A-26 Invader. First the B-25 Mitchell. This most successful of warplanes had a production run of nearly 11,000 airframes serving both the USAAF and the United States Navy. A total of some 700 was used by that service under the designation PBJ.

The Mitchells' most famous operation during the war was that commanded by the then Lt-Col Jimmy Doolittle. This consisted of sixteen B-25Bs operating from the aircraft carrier USS *Hornet* bombing Tokyo in April 1942. The aircraft could not of course return to the carrier not being equipped with arrester gear and so flew on to China where they force-landed or crashed, but fortunately most of the crews survived. For leading this raid, which did much to boost morale in a low point in the Pacific war, Doolittle was awarded the highest medal for valour in America, the Congressional Medal of Honor. After its long wartime service the Mitchell stayed in uniform until early in 1959 when the last models, the TB-25 pilot trainers were retired from Reese Air Force Base in Texas. The B-25 was powered by two Wright R2600 1,700hp radial piston engines.

The first water bomber conversions were made in 1960 carrying a load of 900 gallons. These first conversions were not a success following a number of crashes, the aircraft breaking up after severe manoeuvres following the load drop. They were withdrawn. Later conversions proved to be safer as at the present time a number are still in service in Canada with G & M Aircraft of St Albert, Alberta. How long they will survive before being snapped up by the Warbird movement is hard to say.

The second bomber still in service today, the A-26 Invader, had the distinction of operating in three wars: World War Two, Korea, and then Vietnam. With such a long operational life it is of no surprise that many airframes were available for water bomber conversion. Most conversions had a 1,200-gallon tank with the aircraft being powered by two Pratt & Whitney R2800 radial piston engines. The Invader served with a number of companies in America and Canada. One of the largest Canadian operators of air tankers is Conair of Abbotsford, British Columbia, employing as part of its fleet no less than eight A-26 Invaders into the late 1980s. When they were disposed of some were to head for flying or static museums, but others were sold on to other operators to carry on their trade. The largest A-26 operator today is without doubt Airspray (1967) Ltd of Edmonton and Red Deer, Alberta, employing a staggering eighteen aircraft. One of the current American operators, Lynch Flying Tankers of Billings, Montana, had its Invaders become film stars for the 1989 Steven Spielberg epic *Always*. The film is about water bomber pilots, and as well as starring several Invaders features a Consolidated PBY Catalina and a Fairchild C-119 Boxcar. The film was shot in real water bomber country at locations in Montana and Washington.

Navy patrol aircraft are designed to have a long range and to carry a useful load for that distance. It follows that the type would be ideal for the conversion to tankers. The longevity of the airframe life has meant that examples of most American maritime patrol aircraft designs of the last fifty-plus years are soldiering on to this day.

The Lockheed PV2 Harpoon is not used a great deal today as an air tanker, although examples are stored in Arizona and could be brought up to flying condition fairly quickly. The design dates back to 1943 and was developed from the smaller Lockheed Hudson. It has a powerplant of two 2,000hp Pratt & Whitney R2800 radial piston engines, and the tank capacity for the type is 1,000 gallons. The PV2 Harpoon is one of the American east coast water bombers. Because the climate is much wetter than in the far west there have been traditionally far fewer operators here. One operator with east coast contracts is Hirth Air Tankers of Buffalo, Wyoming which operates six of the type. They contract to both the South Carolina Forestry Commission and the Westavo Corporation to cover managed forests of pine trees; the area planted runs to over 1,000,000 acres and is used for the production of paper products.

The season of high risk is very early, from January to the beginning of April. The season then moves north to Pennsylvania where the State Bureau of Forestry has contracts until mid-May. The contract for Pennsylvania is a prized one as it runs for three years rather than a single year.

The Consolidated PBY Catalina is an amphibian and had the largest product run of any flying boat with a total of over 3,000 being built. This dual role has also meant it has taken a similar position in the world of air tanking: some are operated from land bases and will drop the chemical retardant from either an 800-or a 1,000-gallon tank. The other role is that of dropping water, and to do this task it will operate in an area with a lot of lakes. The Canadian PBYs, or Cansos as they were known, usually operate in this way. What happens is that the pilot descends to skim the surface of the lake and whilst doing so lowers two scoops into the water; these channel the water into the tanks, and when these are full the pilot climbs off the lake surface to drop the water on the fire and then repeats the process. In a 2,000-foot run along a lake in fifteen seconds 800 gallons of water can be scooped up. The PBY can still be found in service in America, Canada, Chile and Spain.

Another Consolidated design is the PB4Y-2 Privateer. Work on this started in May 1943 when a number of PB4Y-1 Liberator bombers were converted into the prototypes of the new model known as the Privateer. The main and most noticeable difference was the installation of a tall single fin to replace the two fins of the PB4Y-1 Liberator. As well as the fin change, the fuselage was lengthened and different engine nacelles fitted. Powering this new type were four Pratt & Whitney R1830-94 radial piston engines of 1,350hp. The new engine had no turbo superchargers fitted since it was designed as a maritime patrol bomber, therefore spending most of its time at low altitudes and not in the thin air at 30,000 feet where the Liberators operated in their bombing of Germany. The total build for the type was 736, and after World War Two service the US Navy operated Privateers in the Korean war; the task required was to drop flares over road convoys so as to illuminate the scene. This having been done, US Marine Corps fighter bombers accompanying the mission would dive and attack the enemy trucks. The Privateer could carry over 150 of the flares.

Whilst US Navy Privateers were operating in Korea, not many miles to the west in French Indo-China the type was entering service with the air arm of the French Navy, the Aéronavale. They were used from 1950 through to the end of French rule in Indo-China in 1954. This rule came to an abrupt end with the defeat of the French Army at the Battle for Dien Bien Phu in May of that year. Following this French Indo-China was split up into the separate nations of Laos, Cambodia and North and South Vietnam. Peace did not return to the area for nearly twenty years until the end of the American withdrawal from Vietnam in the early part of 1975.

Back in the USA the last stand for the military Privateer was that of air-to-air missile target drone under the designation QP-4B. These aircraft were painted bright red and operated from the US Navy Pacific Missile Test Center at Point Magu in California. The last aircraft was destroyed in January 1964.

It was in the early 1960s that the Privateer was first converted to the role of water bomber. The bomb bay tank held 2,400 gallons of retardant. The largest user of the type in the air attack role is Hawkins & Powers of Grey Bull in Wyoming. At the time of writing they have a fleet of five that can be found on station in the western United States and Alaska.

The Hawkins & Powers Privateers have all been re-engined, the original Pratt & Whitneys being replaced by Wright Cyclone R2600 1,700hp radial piston engines. These engines give better performance in the operations in forests at higher altitudes. The extra power is particularly of use on hot days where the air is thin. The operator plans to use the type indefinitely as they have both supplies of spares for the airframes and a large stock of spare Wright Cyclone engines.

The latest two designs used by the US Navy as patrol aircraft have both come from the drawing boards of the Lockheed corporation. These are the P-2V Neptune and the P-3 Orion. The P-2V Neptune formed the backbone of the US Navy's patrol squadrons from 1947 until the mid-1960s. First flown in May 1947 it was powered by two Wright R3350 radial piston engines of 2,300hp. By the time of the last service model, the P-2V7, the horsepower of the R3350s had been raised to 3,500 and a pair of 3,400lb thrust Westinghouse J34 turbojets had been added under the wings.

It was in the late 1970s that the USFS developed the P-2 Neptune as a water bomber. Two companies have followed on from this but have gone down two separate roads. Aero Union of Chico, California, which operates a total of thirteen airframes (not all converted yet), have a very smooth aerodynamic conversion first operated in 1987 with the 2,000-gallon tank fitting almost flush into the lower fuselage. The jet engines have been removed. South of them in New Mexico is Black Hills Aviation in Alamogordo. The conversions here have a more pronounced tank under the fuselage. This is a six-door tank of 2,450 gallons capacity. The Westinghouse jet engines have been retained. Black Hills have a fleet of nine P-2 Neptunes plus a few airframes not yet converted. As it is a relatively new type to this role it can look forward to many years of operations.

The Lockheed P-3 Orion is still the standard US Navy patrol aircraft. It has been in service for thirty years now and no replacement is yet decided upon. The airframes have of course been updated and the very oldest aircraft pensioned off.

It is the model P-3As that have been converted to the newest water bomber type. The P-3A is powered by four Allison T56A turboprops of 4,500 shaft horsepower. This new type of powerplant brings a whole new sound across the forests of America. The turboprop has a lower fuel cost which naturally makes it more popular with the operators. Jet turbine fuel (AVTUR) is also far more freely available than aviation gasoline (AVGAS) used for piston-engined types. The Orion, with a 3,000-gallon load, began to enter service in the early 1990s.

An aircraft that has found a complete new lease of life as a water bomber is the Grumman S2 Tracker. First flown in December 1952 it entered service with the US Navy as a carrier-borne anti-submarine aircraft in February 1954. The design was very successful with over 1,200 examples being built, including licence production of 100 aircraft by de Havilland of Canada for the Royal Canadian Navy. Trackers also served with the air forces and navies of the following countries: Argentina, Australia, Brazil, Italy, Japan, Korea, Holland, Peru, Taiwan, Thailand, Turkey, Uruguay and Venezuela.

The firefighting career of the Tracker began in 1970 in Canada with an ex-RCN aircraft modified by Field Aviation for the Ontario Ministry of Natural Resources. This experiment was found to be successful and eleven other

HV Flying Service C-119 N13742 waits for the call to arms at Santa Barbara CA.

Ex-Canadian Air Force C-119 receives attention at Hawkins & Powers base at Grey Bull, Wyoming.

airframes were converted. In 1978 Conair of Abbotsford, British Columbia converted the first of what was to be the most successful of all Tracker conversions. This aircraft is now usually known as a Conair Firecat. The conversion takes the form of stripping out the surplus military equipment and the fitting of an 870-gallon four-door tank system flush with the lower fuselage. In the USA large numbers of Trackers have been converted by the various operators.

These conversions usually have an 800-gallon tank. With large numbers converted and many airframes stored to await conversion, the type will be in service for many years to come. The Tracker has been modified to take turboprop engines, and conversions to this powerplant continue. The first one converted was designated S2 Turbo and registered N426DF. It was a former US Navy aircraft, TS-2A Bu. No. 133245, first flown by Marsh Aviation of Mesa, Arizona late in November 1986, and it was tested by the California Department of Forestry during the 1988 season from its station at Fresno in California's Central Valley. The conversion removed the two Wright R1820 radial piston engines of 1,525hp and replaced them with Garret TPE331 turboprops of 1,250shp driving a five-blade propeller. In Canada Conair are also going turboprop. There, conversion is powered by two Pratt & Whitney 1,424shp PT6A powerplants. Besides the cheaper cost of fuel the turboprop gives a better performance on one engine, more power in hot and high locations and, last but not least, it is quieter and therefore imposes less strain on the crew.

The most logical type of aircraft to convert to the water bomber role would be a cargo aircraft; after all, it has a large empty fuselage to fit a tank into and it is designed to carry a heavy load a long distance. Surprisingly this has not followed in real life. The first conversion of a cargo plane was in 1957 when a Fairchild C-82 Packet was fitted with a 2,000-gallon tank. The Packet was a twin-boom transport aircraft with the cargo hold in the box-like fuselage. First flown in 1944 and entering service with the US Army Air Force early in 1946, power was provided by two 2,100hp Pratt & Whitney R2800 radial piston engines. As an air attack water bomber it was not a success.

The design was developed into the larger Fairchild C-119 Boxcar, power for this type being provided by two 3,500hp Wright R3350 radial piston engines; later models had a jet boost with the addition of two General Electric J85 turbojets of 2,850lb static thrust, one under each wing. The aircraft converted to water bombing usually had just one jet located above the fuselage. With the jet pack a load of 2,400 gallons was carried; without this boost to power, the load went down to 1,800 gallons. One advantage of the type was that despite having a tank fitted to the middle of the cargo hold there was still room to carry a useful load as a cargo plane. The main user of the type was Hemet Valley Flying Service of California who used it until the early 1980s when it was withdrawn from use following questions over the safety of the type. In Wyoming, Hawkins & Powers brought back from Canada a fleet of ex-RCAF C-119s, but they largely remained unconverted in store at Grey Bull.

The Fairchild C-123 Provider was a powered development of the Chase XG-20 cargo glider; the engines fitted were two 2,300hp Pratt & Whitney R2800 radial piston engines. Later models (C-123K) were fitted with two General Electric J85 turbo jets of 2,850lb static thrust. During its military service, which ran on until the early 1980s, the type received a lot of unwanted attention over its role as a spray aircraft. Thirty-four C-123Ks were modified to UC-123K standard and fitted with underwing spray bars. These aircraft flew across the jungles of Vietnam spraying the highly toxic 'agent orange' to defoliate the trees and thus deprive the enemy, the Vietcong, of cover in their natural environment. TBM Inc of California acquired three aircraft in the early 1980s for conversion to water bombers. Only one was converted to take a 2,000-gallon tank. It was used for a couple of seasons and then retired to the Pima County Aircraft Museum in Tucson, Arizona. The other two aircraft remain in store at Dinuba-Sequoia airfield in California.

The Boeing C-97 transport aircraft was first flown in November 1944. The most widespread use of the type was in its role as a flying refuelling tanker for the USAF, with nearly 600 being built as KC-97Gs. In the mid-1960s a number of aircraft had a General Electric J47 jet engine of

5,200lb static thrust fitted to each wing; these became KC-97Ls and served with the Air National Guard until the type was withdrawn from service in 1977. It was from this stock of tanker aircraft that a number of C-97s were purchased by several operators. Only one has been put into service with a 3,000-gallon tank, this being operated by Hawkins & Powers of Grey Bull, Wyoming. The other aircraft are either stored or operated as freight aircraft.

It is interesting to note that in 1961 a C-97 was fitted with a 4,500-gallon tank and tested in California. Despite having a massive load to drop it proved to be too large to operate in some of the confined spaces required, and also too expensive for that time. Power for the C-97 was provided by four Pratt & Whitney R4360 radial piston engines of 3,500hp each.

The latest transport aircraft to be converted is the Lockheed C-130 Hercules. This is today's most successful military transport aircraft. First flown in August 1954 the type is still in production for the world's air forces. The early model C-130A powered by four Allison T56A turboprops of 3,750shp has largely been withdrawn from service with the USAF, and so a number of aircraft have been converted to the role of water bombers for the 1990s. Fitted with a 4,000-gallon tank, these aircraft are serving with a number of operators and because of their cheaper operating costs will become the standard bomber for the next decade at least. The US Air National Guard has for some years been able to use its C-130s in a firefighting role. This is achieved by fitting a pallet into the rear of the aircraft containing 3,000 gallons of retardant and downward-facing nozzles to dump the load. The system is known as MAFFS (Modular Airborne Fire Fighting System). It was developed by the FMC Corporation of San José, California and was first tested at Edwards Air Force Base in July 1971. The Air Guards would usually be brought in to augment the contracted firefighters during a busy fire season in their own state.

The Douglas DC series of four-engined airliners has proved to be amongst the most successful of the water bomber conversions. The DC-4/-6/-7s are all still in use to this day.

The DC-7 was the first of the 'DC' water bombers by accident. During a test flight of the prototype, N301AA c/n 44122, in the summer of 1953 the crew dumped 1,300 gallons of water ballast over Palm Springs airport. This produced a swathe 200 feet wide and nearly one mile long. The Los Angeles County Fire Department decided to use the aircraft for a number of tests in December of that year, fitting the aircraft with six 400-gallon tanks to give a load of 2,400 gallons, fed through nozzles and not through tanks with doors. The air drop tests took place at Rosamund Dry Lake in Californa. Although the tests proved to be successful, work did not go ahead with the project. The prime reason for this was cost. The DC-7 was at the time 'state of the art' in propliners and far too expensive to sit around waiting for a fire that may not happen. Twenty years later it was a different story and the aircraft was largely unwanted. T & G Aviation of Chandler-Memorial airfield in Arizona are the leaders in DC-7 conversions operating six with a number of airframes awaiting conversion.

Butler Aircraft Company of Redmond, Oregon operate three of the type. The tank is a 3,000-gallon one fitted externally to the underside of the fuselage. Power for the DC-7 comes from four Wright R3350 radial piston engines of 3,250hp each.

The DC-6 airliner first flew in February 1946 at Santa Monica in California. It proved to be the ultimate in piston power with regard to cost and efficiency. To this day, many DC-6s can be found flying as cargo aircraft. So successful was it as a cargo type that it was too expensive an airframe to buy for the limited use and flying of water bombers. Despite that, a number of aircraft were converted. The tank fitted varied from company to company but was in the range of 2,400 gallons to 3,000 gallons. Sis-Q of Santa Rosa, California was a heavy user of the DC-6 in the aerial tanker role. A number of companies gained DC-6s, or rather the military version, the C-118, by swapping old Warbirds with the USAF for museums. This ultimate piston version was powered by four Pratt & Whitney R2800 radials of 2,500hp each.

The first of the DCs in the four-engine configuration was the DC-4, first flown in February 1942 from Santa Monica. The type did sterling work during World War Two under its military designation of C-54, and after the war as purpose-built DC-4 airliners. At the present time the DC-4/C-54 can still be found in military service in the world, and also employed as cargo planes. In the water bomber role the conversions have been of two main types: one is the Ralco conversion which can be spotted by its angular tank, whilst the other is the Aero Union conversion. This features a more aerodynamic tank. The conversions by Aero Union are very highly thought of in the water bombing world. Both have a capacity of 2,000 gallons. The first conversions took place during the mid-1970s and over two dozen aircraft have been modified. Powered by four Pratt & Whitney R2000 radial piston engines of 1,450hp each, the DC-4/C-54 has proved to be one of the most popular and reliable water bombers of recent years.

Two more modern airliners that have competed head to head in the airliner sales market could well end up in the same competition in the water bomber market, albeit thirty years later. These two are the Fokker F27 Friendship and the Avro (Hawker Siddeley) 748, both powered by Rolls-Royce Dart turboprops. The Friendship was first converted in the mid-1980s by Conair of Abbotsford and registered C-GSFS c/n 10473. The aircraft had a 1,680-gallon underslung tank with the pressurisation system removed to avoid complications. The first aircraft went on trial to the Sécurité Civile in France but was unfortunately destroyed in a crash at La Grande Combe near Aries, France in September 1989; since then two others have been converted and operated in France. The Hawker Siddeley 748 was first converted for Macavia at Cranfield, Bedfordshire in England during 1987. It had a higher uplift capacity than the F27, being able to carry 2,000 gallons. Up to now only one aircraft has been converted, G-BNJK c/n 1594.

It remains to be seen whether or not either design is converted to water bombing in any numbers. Both F27s and 748s are still in service as airliners and the unit cost of second-hand airframes may prove too high against competition from military surplus P-3 Orions or C-130 Hercules.

Canada is unique in the world of water bombers as it has produced the only purpose-built water bomber, the Canadair CL-215. The genesis of this design dates back to December 1963 when a symposium comprising forest protection firemen and operators discussed the ideal water bomber aircraft. Canadair designed the CL-215 around the recommendations of that meeting. The aircraft that evolved was an amphibious flying boat powered by two Pratt & Whitney R2800 radial piston engines of 2,100hp each. These engines are very well proven, powering such types as the Douglas DC-6.

The CL-215 could have its 1,600-gallon capacity tanks filled by one of three ways. The first was to fill them with a chemical fire retardant premixed at a ground base, as commonly used by most types of bomber in the USA. The second method was for retardants to be mixed with water scooped in. The last method was for the aircraft to skim across the lake and fill its tanks with plain water. To use this method, and it is the most used method due to the high number of lakes available in the forest areas, the aircraft has scoops under the hull to collect water off a lake as the aircraft skims the surface. In a 4,000-foot run over ten seconds the tanks can be filled up. The drop can be delivered in one second and this will cover an area forty feet wide by 350 feet long. The CL-215 was first flown in October 1967 and made its first water landings the following May.

In Canada the various provinces look after the bulk of firefighting and are therefore able to finance the costs of new purpose-built aircraft with possible low utilisation. Work is also of course contracted out but it is only the provinces that operate 'new' aircraft. Flying Fireman of Vancouver Island claim to be able to operate a fleet of eight PBY Canso/Catalinas for a season at the same cost as one CL-215. This is due to the costs of acquisition and depreciation of a new expensive aircraft as opposed to the cost of a fleet that has been written down in book value over a lot of years.

Despite this the provinces report cost savings. In some years the cost of timber saved more than outweighs the operating and acquisition costs. The productivity of the type is truly amazing. In the province of Quebec one CL-215 made thirty-one pick-ups and drops in one hour. It would have to be assumed that the fire was near the lake! In one day a CL-215 operated by the government of the then Yugoslavia made 225 pick-ups and drops in one day, collecting and dumping over 300,000 gallons of water. The latest design from Canadair is the CL-215T. The 'T' is for turboprop, and the model features a pair of Pratt & Whitney PW123AF engines of 2,380shp. The type is due to enter service in the province of Quebec in 1994, but prior to that two piston-engined examples have been converted to turbines and are operated in that province.

The Canadian operation of having the provinces lead in firefighting has meant that the main bases are quite impressive and feature many high-tech systems. At Dryden HQ in the province of Ontario is a lightning counter. This plots all lightning strikes on a video screen with paper printouts. It is colour co-ordinated to show a period of twenty-four hours. From this can be judged what areas are at a high risk. The count can run into the thousands over a fairly large area.

Canada is home to the most magnificent of all the water bombers, the mighty Martin JRM Mars. The type was ordered for the US Navy in August 1938 and first flown in July 1942. Only five JRM-1s and one JRM-2 with a higher weight were built. The JRM-1s were modified to this higher

RIGHT:
Head-on of HV Flying Service C-119 at home base at Hemet Valley CA.

OPPOSITE:
A-26 Invader N4818E of Lynch Flying Tankers at Billings, Montana. Note spray bars are fitted under the wings.

weight and designated JRM-3. These aircraft were powered by four Wright R3350 radial piston engines of 2,300hp each.

In 1959 a consortium of logging companies under the leadership of MacMillan Bloedel Ltd formed Forest Industries Flying Tankers Ltd. They purchased the four surviving Mars and a large supply of spares for the airframes and over thirty spare engines. Conversion to water bomber was undertaken by Fairey Aviation in Canada. This largest of the water bombers has of course the largest load: 6,000 gallons can be carried. The method of uplift is the same as that of the CL-215; scoops under the fuselage fill the tanks in twenty-two seconds. The size of the Mars is huge: it has a wingspan of 200 feet, a length of 120 feet, and a height of forty-eight feet, with a gross weight of 162,000lb. The four aircraft have been reduced to two – one crashed in 1960 and another was damaged beyond repair in a typhoon in 1962. The two survivors are known as Philippine Mars and Hawaii Mars and are based at Sproat Lake at Port Alberni on Vancouver Island, British Columbia.

The area around here has vast reaches of water so the Mars can scoop and drop for up to five-and-a-half hours on station. The area covered by a drop is 250 feet wide by 800 feet long, or three to four acres. Forest Industries plan to use the Mars for many years to come, and when they are finally grounded (or should that be watered?) they will find homes in museums. The US Navy museum at Pensacola in Florida would be more than keen to get their hands back on the largest flying boat ever operated by that service.

Europe has a small contingent of water bomber operators. These are based around the Mediterranean regions of Greece, Spain and France. All of these are government operators: the national air force in Greece and Spain, and the Sécurité Civile in France. This was founded by the Ministry of the Interior in June 1963 and operated PBY Catalinas. They were one of the launch customers for the Canadair CL-215, ordering a total of fifteen.

The French have worked both with manufacturers and operators in Canada. With Canadair they have ordered twelve examples of the CL-215T for delivery from 1994. With Conair they have operated the Firecat. Currently they have a total of fifteen: nine piston-engined and six turbopowered. Over the next few years this will change as the piston-powered examples are re-engined to form an all turbine fleet. Two American operators, T & G and Hemet Valley Flying Services have leased examples of the C-130 Hercules to the Sécurité Civile. If successful then they are likely to acquire a stock, as their own fleet is lacking at the 'heavy' end of the bombers since the phasing out of the Douglas DC-6 fleet in the late 1980s.

Water bombers, whilst changing towards turbopower, will still provide for many years yet the sound of 'pounding pistons' and the sight of aircraft that cannot be seen anywhere else in the world doing a vital job in protecting the environment. Truly they are the 'greenest' aircraft around.

ABOVE:
Conair Invader Tanker No. 21 at the home base of Abbotsford BC.

RIGHT:
Film star A-26 N9425Z of Lynch Flying Tankers. This aircraft No. 57 starred in the Steven Spielberg epic *Always*.

28

The sole C-123 converted by TBM as a water bomber. Seen here at Stockton CA.

Two hot-rod bombers; F7F Tigercats of TBM Inc of Dinuba-Sequoia. Both of these aircraft have since been snapped up by museums.

ABOVE:
Biggest of the land-based bombers, Boeing C-97G N1365N of Hawkins & Powers at Grey Bull WY.

LEFT:
TBM Avengers N7226C & N6447C in late evening sun at Shafter CA.

ABOVE:
Grumman Tracker converted to Conair Firecat. Aircraft C-GWUP Tanker No. 68 at Abbotsford BC.

RIGHT:
P-2V7 Neptune N14447 of Black Hills Aviation at Alamogordo, New Mexico. Note conversion to water bomber retains underwing jets.

LEFT:
Aero Union Neptune conversion N701AU at its Chico base. This very smart conversion removes the underwing jets.

BELOW:
Under a clear Arizona sky Evergreen Aviation Neptune N202EV at Marana HQ.

ABOVE:
B-17 N17W of Globe Air, Tanker No. 04 at Porterville CA. The historic value of this aircraft has exceeded its tanker value and it is now owned by the Museum of Flight at Boeing Field, Seattle WA.

RIGHT:
Chico California was home to most of the surviving Grumman AF2S Guardians. Tanker No. 21 N9995Z is seen here.

LEFT:
C-54 Skymaster C-GBNV of Conifair at St Jean, Quebec. Note overwing spray bars for insect control.

BELOW:
Not a Russian water bomber but Aero Union DC-4 N708Z painted up for a role in the John Travolta film *The Experts*. Seen back at Chico after filming.

RIGHT:
Aero Union DC-4 N76AU fitted with that company's slick tank conversion at Lancaster CA.

BELOW:
European water bomber in the guise of Sécurité Civile DC-6 F-ZBAE seen here at Paris-Le Bourget.

ABOVE:
Douglas DC-7C N90802 of T&G framed under the wing of another of the same type at Chandler AZ.

LEFT:
Wenatchee-Pangborn in Washington state hosts Sis-Q DC-6 N888SQ.

ABOVE:
Most PV2 Harpoon tankers are in store. N7086C is at Chandler AZ.

RIGHT:
Turboprop-powered by a pair of Rolls-Royce Dart engines is Conair's first F27 conversion Tanker No. 27 (what else?) at Abbotsford BC.

Flying Fireman operated a fleet of eight PBY Catalinas. Tanker No. 3 C-FFFZ is parked at Sidney, Vancouver Island.

The only purpose-built water bomber is the Canadian CL-215. Running its P & W R2800 piston engines is Tanker No. 263 at Ontario Province HQ at Dryden.

Air Caledonia PBY-5A Catalina on a lay-over at Vancouver. This aircraft, C-FJCV, was later sold to Zimbabwe as Z-CAT where it conducted air safaris throughout Africa. Since then it has moved to New Zealand.

PLEASURE FLYING

To the average man in the street the thought of flying in an aeroplane that is fifty years old would fill him with absolute horror. To the enthusiast, the reaction to the prospect of such a flight would simply be 'Where do I book from?'

The propliner workhorse has the same effect on many people, as does the steam engine on the real railway buff. The noise that assails the eardrums, the smoke that blinds the view when the engine starts up, and the vibration throughout the aircraft that is transmitted through every nerve in the passenger's body are not negative effects upon the passenger, but the very reason for the trip: to try to recreate the days when air travel was an adventure for only a rich and privileged few.

The most favoured aircraft used for this type of pleasure flight is the venerable Douglas DC-3 Dakota. This aircraft just simply goes on and on and no replacement has ever been able to take over all its roles. In the early 1960s a number of different manufacturers were building what were described as Dakota replacements. These included the Fokker F27 Friendship, the Handley Page Herald and the Avro (now BAe) 748. All good aircraft, all still in service today; in fact two of the designs have been upgraded to new aircraft, the Fokker 50 and the BAe ATP. However, more than one air carrier continues to replace an old DC-3 with a newer one or one with fewer flying hours on the airframe.

With this background it is easy to see why all over the world it is possible to enjoy the delights of aerial nostalgia in Douglas's elegant design. The most publicised trips in Dakotas belong to Vintage Air Tours of Orlando, Florida. Part of Richard Branson's Virgin group, the company operated two Dakotas on a scheduled service from Kissimmee to Key West, the southernmost part of Florida. The flight was a trip back in time to May 1945, to the day the war ended in Europe. The pilots and cabin crew wore period uniforms and the inflight magazines were all from this date. The flights were very popular with the passengers, but regrettably not enough people flew with them and in October 1994 the operation was closed down. Besides Florida it is possible to enjoy the Dakota on America's west coast as two operators run trips: Otis Spunkmeyer Air have two aircraft based at Oakland, California, and Classic Airlines of Spokane, Washington have a single example.

Europe does not lack for such flights as they can be enjoyed in Sweden with Flygande Veteraner, in Holland with the Dutch Dakota Association, in Norway with Dakota Norway, in Finland with Air Veteran OY, in Switzerland with Classic Air, and in the United Kingdom with Air Atlantique. This company operates a number of different types of flight from a charter to go to an airshow by air. When the aircraft has arrived it will then usually operate a number of around-the-area flights for visitors to the show, and at the end of the day it will fly back to base with the original set of passengers. The other method of flying is for the aircraft to go to an airfield to operate sightseeing flights over a particular event. For example the arrival in a city of the 'tall ships' will bring out the crowds; what better way to see the ships than to fly over them when they are out at sea with their sails up?

Down under in Australia flights are operated by such carriers as Dakota Airways, Dakota Down Under, DC-3 Australia, Desert Air Safaris, Air North and Short Stop Jet Charter which, despite its name, operates dinner flights over the city of Melbourne.

In South America the Dakota can be found to be a hard-working cargo and passenger aircraft. Venezuela has two airlines taking tourists to see one of the wonders of the world, Angel Falls on Auyantepuy in the Guyana highlands. With a drop of 3,200 feet, Angel Falls is the world's tallest falls. It was not named after any heavenly being but after Jimmie Angel, an American pilot looking for gold in the region, who landed his aeroplane on the Mesa in 1937. This aeroplane, a Ryan Flamingo, can be see to this day on display outside the terminal building at Ciudad Bolivar airport.

The two airlines Servivensa and Rutaca will fly from Ciudad Bolivar and perform a sightseeing tour of the Falls and the surrounding area, landing either at the small airport at Canaima or on the strip at Kavac. Here lunch will be served followed by a walk under a waterfall in this most beautiful part of South America. So remote is this area that some years ago a Dakota on a tour of Angel Falls lost an engine; that is to say, it fell off! The pilot managed to crash-land the aircraft without any injuries to the passengers or crew, but because of its location the aircraft is still where it landed today. Some tours even overfly it and its story is told.

Today the sea-plane or flying boat is only to be found in a few locations around the world. Places with small island communities are natural locations to be connected by such an air service, the Caribbean islands and the Bahamas group of islands both fitting the bill for this operation.

In the Bahamas, Chalk's International are the airline to travel with if you want to see all the islands. The airline can claim to be one of the world's oldest, being founded in 1919. It is based at Watson Island SPB (Sea-Plane Base) in Miami, Florida. Two types of aircraft are operated, the main one being the Grumman G-73 Mallard. This is a twin-engine high-wing monoplane with a boat-like hull and a retractable undercarriage so that the type is a true amphibian. The prototype Mallard was first flown in April 1946. Power was supplied by two Pratt & Whitney Wasp nine-cylinder air-cooled radials of 550hp. This made the type underpowered. In later years many have been converted to turbo Mallards by the fitting of two Pratt & Whitney (Canada) PT6A engines of 650shp. The production run of the Mallard was short with only fifty-nine being built before manufacture was terminated in May 1951.

The other type of flying boat operated by Chalk's is the Grumman HU-16 Albatross. This design is a big brother to the Mallard and had a far longer production run with 466 being built, the first in September 1947 and the last in May 1961. Most Albatrosses were built for military service, being used as an air-sea rescue aircraft with the US Air Force, the US Navy and the US Coast Guard. The type was operated in twenty-two other countries around the world.

Civil conversions of ex-military aircraft under the designation G-111 were first flown in February 1979 and first operated by Chalk's in October 1981. Most of the conversions were soon in storage at the Pinal Air Park, Marana, in Arizona. At the time of writing Chalks are only operating one G-111 Albatross in a thirty-seat configuration.

What is it like for the passengers to fly on one of these operations? The answer is a very relaxed, no-stress way to travel. The check-in for flight BK300 to Bimini at the Chalks terminal on Paradise Island, Nassau in the Bahamas is quite the easiest anywhere in the world. With only a total of thirteen to seventeen seats to fill on a flight the small terminal does not get full. The airline will operate both schedule services and ad hoc charters to the various islands of the Bahamas and so a number of flights may be being operated at any one time. No boarding cards are issued to the passengers; 'We know everyone' says the cheerful station manager.

Boarding G-73 Mallard N73556 is simple and the seats are all very comfortable, and with the aircraft having a high wing the view from the windows is excellent. Last on is the co-pilot who shuts the door, no flight attendant being carried. He gives the flight safety briefing as he walks up the aisle to the cockpit: 'No smoking please during the flight; please note the position of the exits; your lifejacket is under your seat; and please fasten your seat belt...' Pardon? I didn't quite catch all that. Never mind, I think I know what he was saying. The engines start with a cloud of smoke and then settle down to a rhythmic throb. The brakes are released and we taxi across the apron down the ramp into the water. A long taxi takes the Mallard under the bridge connecting Nassau and Paradise Island to the beginning of the take-off run. I look out of the window and see a man on a cabin cruiser taking a photograph; the blue and white flying boat must look very nice in that setting.

The power is increased for the take-off and water obscures the windows as the flying boat races through the water. The noise level from the two piston engines is very

high and the take-off seems to go on for ever. But soon the aircraft lifts off the water and the windows are once again clear. The view over Paradise Island, the beach, and the hotels is spectacular. The Mallard heads for Bimini and flies along at two thousand feet giving a wonderful view over the small islands and the shipping that cross our route on the fifty-minute flight.

The runway at Bimini must be one of the most scenic in the world, a small sand bar with palm trees on one side and Bimini with its small hotels, shops and fishing boats on the other. The landing in a flying boat is very smooth and the first indication that you have landed is when the water flies past the window and obscures the view. The arrival on dry land is surprising. The aircraft after it has landed lowers its undercarriage (that must be an odd sensation for a pilot) and taxis up a ramp out of the water. The aircraft taxis across the main road – there are no signs of traffic lights to warn approaching vehicles – and parks outside the International Arrivals terminal, a medium-size hut bordered by palm trees.

We passengers have a few hours to spend on Bimini and so decide to go for a walk across the island. This takes about five minutes as we find Bimini is long but very narrow. A walk along the length of the island is then taken. Bimini is known as the game fishing capital of the world, and the number of boats for hire and large stuffed fish in the bars add to this claim. With the time for the second leg of the flight due we return to the International Departure terminal, the same small hut. A total of six people has checked in for flight BK104 to Miami. Mallard N2442H arrives from Nassau to operate this sector.

It produces a wonderful photograph as it taxis out of the water and up the ramp. Turnaround is quick and all too soon we are racing down the scenic runway for the twenty-minute flight in late afternoon to Miami. Miami Beach with its high-rise hotels and long sandy beaches soon comes into view. The beaches look empty – it must be too hot!

We turn over downtown Miami, cross multi-level road crossovers and head for our aquatic landing strip in the dock area. The landing is much rougher than at Bimini but still smoother than most land planes. Water laps past the windows and showers of spray leap from the wing floats as we taxi to the ramp at Watson Causeway. Sadly we have to deplane and proceed to the small terminal building to clear

RIGHT:
Dornier Do 228 of Aereotuy at Kavac airstrip in Venezuela. This had brought a party of nineteen people to see Angel Falls, the world's highest waterfall.

OPPOSITE:
Rutaca DC-3 YV-218C at Kavac waits for its tourist party to have lunch before the flight home.

US Customs and collect our bags. The immigration procedure is the quickest I have ever had at any US entry port and by far the friendliest. There is a lot to be said for entering a country in such an unusual and out-of-the-way location.

If the Bahamas has scenic flying of one type, then in Switzerland one can enjoy spectacular views of the Alps and experience the thrill of flying in a genuine German-built World War Two aircraft. These are Junkers Ju 52/3m tri-motor transport aircraft. Three aeroplanes were delivered to the Swiss Air Force in October 1939 and all survived their long lives as training aircraft for various airborne tasks and as transport and parachute drop aircraft.

In 1982, after over forty years' service, they were retired from Air Force service. At that time the Swiss Air Force was trying to raise money for a new museum building and decided to operate the Ju 52s for a limited time giving pleasure flights. This was so successful that they decided to make the operation permanent, and so JU-Air was formed to operate all three aircraft. As one would expect of a Swiss-run operation, all the aircraft are in perfect condition and the powerplants of the three BMW 132A3 660hp nine-

cylinder radial engines hum like a well-oiled sewing machine. The cabin interior is for seventeen passengers and everyone has a single seat. The seats are modern and comfortable but the cabin walls are still the stark bare metal, and running along the top of the roof is the wire for parachutists to clip their static lines to. The aeroplane is, of course, unpressurised and so has large windows. As the aircraft flies through, not above the Alps the views are staggering. The crews flying them have many thousands of hours on these aircraft and are totally at home in a mountain environment.

The airline has acquired a fourth aircraft but this is not a real Junkers-built one but a licensed Spanish aircraft built by Casa in 1949. This airframe is under a long-term rebuild at the company's headquarters, the Swiss Air Force base at Dübendorf near Zürich. It is not expected to fly until at least 1996. One can hope that, given Swiss craftsmanship, JU-Air will be flying their tri-motors for many years to come.

For the traveller who yearns to fly in something different from the Boeing 737 in which they go on holiday, if they look out for unusual flights they will not be disappointed by the experience.

RIGHT:
Jumping out of perfectly good aeroplanes is very popular in California. DC-3 N4991E awaits the next band of skydivers at Lodi.

BELOW AND OPPOSITE:
YV-610C Dakota of Servivensa taxis in with a fresh batch of visitors at Kavac. Note the large picture windows for better views of the Falls.

Simply the best way to see Snowdon and the other peaks of North Wales. De Havilland Rapide G-AIDL at its base at Caernarfon.

LEFT:
Now owned by Lufthansa for promotional and pleasure flying, this Ju 52/3m was previously owned by aviation author Martin Caidin. Known as *Iron Annie* it is seen here at Leesburg in Florida registered as N42JU.

BELOW:
Landing at Zürich from a sight-seeing tour of the Alps is JU-Air Junkers Ju 52/3m HB-HOP.

RIGHT:
Scenic Airways of Las Vegas fly to such places as the Grand Canyon. Ford Tri-motor N76GC waits for the next crowd of people fed up with slot machines and casinos.

BELOW:
Ford Tri-motor NC8407 of the Experimental Aircraft Association. The EAA keeps a flying museum and is seen here at the Sun 'n' Fun fly-in at Lakeland FL.

Chalk's International, one of the oldest airlines in the world, founded in 1919, lands Grumman G-73 Mallard N2442H at perhaps the world's most scenic runway, Bimini in the Bahamas.

Line-up of Russia's 'go anywhere carry
anything' Antonov An-2s at Rzhevka near
St Petersburg.

LIFTING THE IRON CURTAIN

During the days of the old Soviet Union the operators of any type of aeroplane were easy to sort out. If it was a military type then it was the Red Air Force. If the operator was civil then it was operated by Aeroflot, the state operation that controlled all civil flying from flying clubs to crop sprayers to international passenger flights.

The failure of the Moscow coup attempt by Gennady Yanayev and his hard-line communist co-conspirators in August 1991 led to the break-up of the old Soviet Union, with all the separate republics that made up the Union going their own way as independent countries. This has left the civil aviation scene in these countries in what could be described as a state of flux. Each of these republics has taken over most of the Aeroflot assets that were on their soil. Some have formed new airlines and started operations both internally and externally from the new country or republic. Others are operating aircraft in the· old Aeroflot colour scheme with the 'CCCP' prefix to the registration being painted out. Eventually some order will come out of this, but until then the type of aircraft, the colour scheme and the registration carried will not be predictable.

The two largest republics are Russia and the Ukraine. Both these republics have a large aircraft manufacturing base. Russia builds the Ilyushin and Tupolev designs whilst the Ukraine builds the Antonov designs.

It is an Antonov design that is the most widely flown of all propliners, the Antonov An-2 (NATO codename Colt). The An-2 is unique as it is the only post-World War Two transport aircraft that is a biplane. The first aircraft flew in August 1947 and subsequent production models were powered by a single ASh-621R air-cooled radial piston engine of nine cylinders producing up to 1,000hp. The cockpit has room for a crew of two but usually only one is used. Seating is for up to twelve people or a mix of passengers and cargo.

The An-2 is one of the 'can go anywhere and can carry anything' types of aircraft. It has a wide-track fixed undercarriage and can be fitted with floats for areas where there are a lot of lakes, or fitted with skis for the long and cold Russian winter. The users of the design range from small airlines to crop sprayers; a 300-gallon load of chemicals can be dispersed by the fitting of underwing spray bars. It can also carry parachutists, a popular pastime in Russia. To operate in this mode the door measuring 5 ft by 4 ft 9 in can be removed to facilitate an easy exit from the aircraft. Other uses include meteorological research, survey work, glider towing and any other operation that can use the An-2 airframe.

Besides production in the Ukraine, An-2s were built in Poland by PZL and also in China. The production run ran into many thousands with the PZL lines in Poland keeping production going until at least the late 1980s, a lifespan of over forty years. This is testimony to a very good design that can do the job required. Sales of the An-2 to the West before the collapse of the Iron Curtain were sparse, but since then a number of people are importing the type at bargain basement prices. The countries of what was once the Warsaw Pact will seemingly sell anything for hard Western currency. At Kiev the Antonov design bureau (OKB) has produced a turboprop version known as the An-3. Like a number of other turboprop versions of workhorses it has not been produced in any numbers.

A large number of Western aircraft have an Eastern bloc equivalent. The Lockheed C-130 Hercules has an opposite number in the Antonov An-12 (NATO codename Cub). Both aircraft have the same high-wing layout and the size of both is similar.

The development of the An-12 can be traced back over two aircraft designs. First is the An-8 (NATO codename Camp). This was a twin-engined high-wing transport aircraft with a box-like fuselage and rear ramp loading. It is believed to have first flown late in 1955 and it made its public debut at the Soviet Aviation Day display at Tushino-Moscow the following June. Power was provided by two Ivchenko AI-20 turboprops of 4,000shp, or two Kuznetov NK6s of similar power output. It was thought at one time that the type had not entered production as it was not widely seen by Western observers. Late in 1993 at least fifty aircraft of this type were listed as being current with Aeroflot or their successors.

Following directly on from the An-8 was the Antonov An-10 Ukraine (NATO codename Cat). This four-engined turboprop was powered by Ivchenko AI-20s of 4,000shp in the production aircraft. The An-10 had the same layout as the cargo An-8 (except for two extra engines) but was in fact an airliner with no cargo door at all. Accommodation varied from an eighty-five-seat to a 110 high density version, and it claimed to be the most economic airliner in the world when it was introduced in the summer of 1959. It is believed that all An-10s are now out of service.

The Antonov An-12 was the logical development of the An-10. This cargo variant had an upswept rear fuselage and a rear loading ramp. First flown in 1958 it entered service in 1960 and went on to form the backbone of the Soviet transport fleet, both civil and military. The aircraft has been exported both to the airlines and the air forces of at least a dozen countries. The An-12 is powered by the same type of units as those fitted to the An-10. The type can be expected to be seen flying for many years to come and will no doubt over the years move down the chain to the independent operators, as has its Western counterpart the Lockheed C-130 Hercules.

As in the West, Soviet designers in the late 1950s were designing a twin-engine turboprop to replace the older piston-engined aircraft. In the West the Fokker F27 Friendship, Handley Page HPR7 Herald and the Avro 748 were all trying to be the Douglas DC-3 Dakota replacement, whilst in the Soviet Union the types to be replaced were the Ilyushin Il-14 (NATO codename Crate) and the Lisunov Li-2 (NATO codename Cab). This latter type was licence-built version of the Dakota. To replace these the Antonov bureau in the Ukrainian capital of Kiev came up with the

An-24 (NATO codename Coke), a high-wing transport passenger aeroplane. Powerplants were two Ivchenko AI-24Vs of 2,550shp each driving a four-blade propeller. The maiden flight was at the end of December 1959 with an entry to service in April 1962. Seating capacity was up to fifty passengers.

Like all good designs, new variants of them have been produced. The first of such was the An-24V series II powered by two Ivchenko AI-24T turboprops of 2,820shp to improve the performance for hot and high airfields. To further aid hot and high performance came the An-24RV. This variant had fitted to the back end of the right-hand engine nacelle a Tumanskii RV19-300 jet engine with a thrust output of 1,980lb. The first variant with a frieght door was the An-24RT. This had a tail opening door which could be opened in flight to allow air drops of cargo by parachute. Since the An-24RT did not have a proper loading ramp with drive-in capability, it did not find favour and so a new version, An-26 (NATO codename Curl), was produced with this deficiency rectified. This aircraft has become the standard light transport aircraft in Aeroflot and in the military.

The version with the highest power is the An-32 (NATO codename Cline). This is fitted with two Ivchenko AI-20M turboprops of 5,180shp, nearly twice the power output of the earlier types. To accommodate this engine a radical re-design of the engine mounts had to be made. The engines are mounted above the wings as opposed to below them to cope with the much larger propeller.

The oddest looking variant was the An-30 (NATO codename Clank), a survey aircraft with a large glazed nose used for photographic surveys for mineral resources in the remote parts of the country. The aircraft retains its cargo capability so that it can operate on its own carrying the equipment, supplies and personnel needed to complete a photographic mission. The first time the An-30 was shown in the West was in 1974 when it appeared at the Hanover Air Show in Germany. In late 1993 Aeroflot was operating a fleet of fifty-seven aircraft of this type, mostly with the polar division working in Siberia.

One of the two types that the An-24 and its developments were built to replace was the Russian Dakota, the Lisunov Li-2. This was a licence-built version of the Douglas workhorse. Before production started in 1940, over twenty Douglas-built aircraft had been sold to the Soviet Union during the previous four-year period. Power for the Li-2 was provided by a number of various engines. The main one used was the Shvetsov ASh-62 air-cooled radial piston engine of 1,200hp. The production run of the Li-2 ran until the end of World War Two, or, as it was known in the Soviet Union, 'The Great Patriotic War'. It has not yet been possible to get an exact figure of the number of aeroplanes built but it has been estimated at between two and three thousand aircraft. The Li-2 was exported to a number of communist countries including China and Vietnam. It is possible that some aircraft may still be in service in either country as they have been sighted as late as the 1980s.

The other type the An-24 series replaced was the Ilyushin Il-14. This aircraft was a direct development of the Soviet Union's first post-war transport aircraft the Ilyushin Il-12 (NATO codename Coach). The Il-14 flew for the first time in 1950 and entered service four years later with both the Red Air Force and Aeroflot. It was an upgrade in performance, safety and reliability over the Il-12. Surprisingly it carried fewer passengers than the previous model but had a longer range. The passenger load of up to twenty-six was later improved to carry an extra ten people. Power was from two Shvetsov ASh-82 air-cooled radial piston engines of 1,900hp driving a four-blade propeller. The aircraft had licenced production in two other countries. The VEB works in Dresden, East Germany built around eighty airframes during the mid to late 1950s. In Czechoslovakia the Avia works in Prague built approximately 120, ending production in 1960. Plans to build the aircraft in China did not come to fruition. The Il-14 can still be found in service in both Russia and China. In Russia it is still in service with the polar division of Aeroflot at its base near Moscow at Myachikovo airfield, albeit in very small numbers. The number in service in China is not known, but all visitors to this country have reported them still flying and in some cases actually carrying passengers.

Like its Western counterparts the Lockheed Electra and the Bristol Britannia, the Ilyushin Il-18 Moskva (NATO codename Coot) was a turboprop in a new age of pure jets. However, in the Soviet Union in the late 1950s and the 1960s passenger opinion was not something that Aeroflot needed to worry about. The traveller flew on whatever type of aircraft was operating on a particular route. If you wanted to fly in a pure jet and an Il-18 was on the flight, then it was either fly or not. The airline had a total monopoly. This situation gave the Il-18 a production run far longer than its Western counterparts. Over 600 aircraft were built in an eleven-year period starting in 1957.

July 1957 saw the first flight of this four-engined airliner. The power was supplied by Ivchenko AI-20 turboprops of 4,000shp each. During its initial airline service the passenger load was variable, but around eighty people was the norm. As with so many airliners, more seats are squeezed in and current aircraft have 100 economy seats. As of late 1993 Aeroflot still list over seventy aircraft in its fleet. Most are in the airline configuration but a number have been converted to research and survey aircraft. These are easily spotted by the extra aerials, pods and other external modifications.

How these few propliner types will survive in Russia and in the other members of the Commonwealth of Independent States is not clear. The countries are in too great a state of flux. Some of the republics are virtually at war with their neighbours. At the end of the day however, all these types do a job that is vital in a geographic area the size of the CIS. As long as that happens, the sound of propellers will be heard over the icy wastes of that massive land mass.

LEFT:
Antonov An-2 CCCP 40488 at Rzhevka. This photograph was taken in August 1991 just days after the coup that led to the break-up of the Soviet Union. Most aircraft now carry 'RA' in place of CCCP in Russia.

BELOW:
Czech-built LET 410UVP CCCP 67106 is one of the newer commuter types to be found in Aeroflot markings.

ABOVE:
Soviet equivalent of the F-27, HS748 and
Herald, the Antonov An-24RV CCCP 46601
at Rzhevka.

RIGHT:
Antonov An-30 is the survey variant of the
An-24, the glass nose giving good views of
the area flown over. CCCP 30023 seen at
Myachikovo near Moscow.

The Ilyushin Il-14 was to the East what the Dakota was to the West. Seen at Myachikovo, CCCP 79162 awaits the scrapman.

Standard eastern bloc medium transport,
this Antonov An-12 CCCP 11029 taxis past
others of the same type at Pulkovo-St
Petersburg.

ABOVE:
Helicopters are of great importance in Russia and have been built in vast numbers. This Mil Mi-2 CCCP 20250 is at Rzhevka.

LEFT:
The Kamov family of helicopters all use the co-axial rotor configuration. Many are used for crop spraying. This Ka-26 is at Rzhevka.

RIGHT:
Only in Colombia will an operator open the emergency exit so you can lean out and take photographs! DC-3 flying near Villavicencio.

BELOW:
Villavicencio is home to many workhorse props. HK3349, a Dakota of Tagua, sits upon the apron.

SOUTH AMERICAN SNAPSHOTS

The continent of South America is home to a very high proportion of the world's workhorse props. The basic reason for this is purely an economic one. Most of the countries of that continent are poor and carry a high debt to the Western banks. Add to this the lack of good road or rail transport systems together with a mountainous terrain in a number of countries, and the only answer of how to transport many essential items is to fly them.

The freight transporters cannot afford to buy new jet equipment or even old first-generation jets such as the Boeing 707 or the Douglas DC-8, so they have bought the propliners that few other people wanted. It costs very little to buy these airframes, engines and spare parts. They are relatively simple to maintain mechanically, and to this can be added the relatively lax airworthiness standards of their governments in terms of airframe and engine maintenance and pilot duty flying hours. The result of this is cheap air transport with no frills but a lot of accidents, some minor but some regrettably major, often involving the total destruction of the aircraft involved and the deaths of the crew and passengers.

Let us look in more detail at a few countries in South America. First is Bolivia. This land-locked country is famous for having revolutions and cocaine. The country was named after Simon Bolivar, the great liberator of South America from the forces of Spanish colonialism. General Sucre liberated the country previously known as Upper Peru at the Battle of Tumulsa in 1825 (the official capital is known after him). It is sad to record that in 160 years of independence the government has been changed seventy-eight times, usually by means of a military coup or revolution.

The usual entry into Bolivia is via La Paz, the commercial and political capital of the country. The airport El Alto is well named due to the fact that it is set upon the Altiplano or high plateau. This is an area approximately eighty-five miles by 520 miles long that runs from south-eastern Peru to south-western Bolivia; 40,000 square miles of the plateau are in Bolivia. It is cold, windswept, treeless and high. The airport is the world's highest at 13,500 feet above sea level. This means that the air is very thin, affecting the performance of aeroplanes, so the runway is a massive 13,000 feet long. The first thing the visitor notices when walking across the tarmac from the incoming flight to the terminal is how thin the air is. This short walk leaves a breathless feeling so that any normal activity such as running up a flight of stairs will have the same effect as running a marathon. It will take several days for the visitor to acclimatise to the height. It is interesting to note that if you are flying in the United Kingdom in an unpressurised aircraft, then at 12,000 feet you should be on oxygen. La Paz finds you walking about, albeit slowly, at 13,500 feet!

Scattered around the wide expanse of the airfield are to be found many derelict and semi-derelict aircraft. Mixed in amongst them are the real live working ones. It is often difficult to spot which is which.

Since most people in Bolivia live in the highlands and most of the agriculture is naturally in the lowlands, the produce for the latter has to be moved to the former. Meat is the main product moved. The handlers of this are known as 'carniceros'. The carriers for this trade usually have only a small number of aircraft, perhaps two or three together with a total staff of about a dozen people. This includes pilots, mechanics, loaders and office staff. Few 'airlines' last more than about five years as owners far too often take most of the profits and invest too little in maintenance of aircraft or engines. The aircraft involved will be a real workhorse.

Medellin may be famous for other things but Sadelca DC-3 HK1212 will take your mind off them.

One of the favourite types used has been the Curtiss C-46 Commando; cheap to buy, cheap to run and able to carry a load of five tons from a 3,000-foot airstrip of gravel or grass. Most aircraft are in a bare metal finish or the paint scheme of a previous operator with one name painted out and the new name painted on. Little regard is given to corporate image or identity. Over seventy-five C-46s have been used in Bolivia over the years. Bolivia has more C-46s flying than any other country. The operators work as follows. An operator has a contract to fly meat from lowland farms to the capital. A flight will depart from La Paz and fly to the farmer's strip. This strip may be of dubious quality and is usually not more than 3,000 feet long. It will contain no navigation aids so flights will be under VFR (Visual Flight Rules) conditions. As the aircraft leaves, a radio message is transmitted to the farm stating that the aircraft is on its way. The cattle are then taken from the fields and slaughtered quickly on site and the carcasses cut up.

The aeroplane arrives and the freshly killed meat is loaded quickly on to the aircraft for its return flight. When it arrives back at La Paz the meat is thrown into the back of a truck and taken to the market in the city. Speed is of the utmost importance as at no stage in the process is refrigeration used. It is not at all unusual to see local peasant women dressed in bowler hats and mutli-layered skirts buying joints of meat straight from the plane. Local dogs, who will lie in a lazy stupor most of the day, will spring into action as well, for when the inside of the aircraft is hosed out or when large bath-like bins for meat transportation are emptied, they are just tipped out of the door on to the dusty ground of the airport. This mixture of water, blood, offal and grease proves an attractive meal for the dogs.

The buildings around the cargo area are a sight to be seen. Mostly old stone and tin shacks, the administrative offices look as they would have done forty years ago with the oldest radios, typewriters and desks you could imagine. Outside on the gravel is the maintenance bay. Hangars are just not used. All work goes on outside from simple jobs to a total rebuild. The Bolivian mechanic is a master of improvisation and can keep almost any piece of machinery going somehow. An aircraft fuselage without wings stacked up on oil drums and blocks of wood is not a scrapped aircraft for spares reclamation but a total rebuild from ground up. It may take a few years to build it up, but time and labour are both cheap. It should be noted, however, that Bolivia has the world's worst air accident record.

To the south-east of La Paz 150 miles away is Bolivia's second city of Cochabamba. The arrival at Jorge Wilstermann airport from La Paz is a relief to the visitor as the airport is only at 8,400 feet. Although by most standards it is still high altitude for an airport, compared to La Paz it is oxygen rich. The cargo flown from here is more of a general kind than that at La Paz, and scattered around the perimeter of the airport are the hangars of operators.

To be found here are such carriers as North-East Bolivian Airlines. Two aircraft are operated by this carrier, a C-46 Commando and a Convair 440 Metropolitan. This latter aircraft was recently rebuilt after what most people would have regarded as a write-off crash. Never say never with

Bolivian aircraft. On a far more upmarket basis is Lineas Aereas Canedo (LAC) operating two Convair 340s. These aircraft came in 1992 to the airline from storage by the USAF at Davis-Monthan Air Force Base in Arizona. Both are maintained to the highest standards and are quite immaculate. Both are for passenger charters, one fitted out as a very comfortable airliner configuration, the other as a VIP executive interior. The airline's owner and one of its pilots, Comd Rolando Canedo Lopez, has a long experience of flying in the area and over the years has operated such types as a Fairchild C-82 Packet and a Douglas DC-3 Dakota.

Cochabamba is home base to Bolivia's national flag carrier, Lloyd Aereo Boliviano, who can claim to be one of the world's oldest airlines having been formed in 1925. Except for two Fokker F27 Friendship turboprop airliners, the fleet is an all-jet operation.

To the north of Bolivia across the equator lies Colombia. The country suffers from two major problems: the left-wing guerrilla fighters and the cocaine barons, both from their own points of view trying to destabilise the elected government. The capital of this country is Bogota at an altitude of 8,700 feet, so once again the air is thin. The airport El Dorado is a feast for the propliner fan as many types can be seen operating next to modern jet equipment. Oil is one of the economies and any oil field needs supplies and workers flown out to it. Douglas DC-3 Dakotas and their big brothers the DC-6s can be seen loading items such as drill shafts for oil wells or many other items of general cargo.

The drug problem has meant that ramp security is high with police and sniffer dogs patrolling the areas. This is not just to stop the carriage of cocaine or marijuana but also to stop aeroplanes being stolen to fly drugs into the USA. Part of the Colombian Air Force ramp at El Dorado is a graveyard of old propliners and some more modern twin turboprops that have been impounded for drug running. The big four-engine Douglas transport usually carries marijuana because it is a bulk cargo compared to value; the twins carry the cocaine, this having a high value to weight.

The system works something like what follows. It must be said that it is not a complete or fully accurate report due to the fact that drug runners do not wish to publish accounts for their activities. Details have been culled from a number of published reports. An aeroplane is either stolen or purchased for a run to the USA. The type will depend upon the type of drug and its weight to be carried: as stated earlier, the two main drugs have vastly different weight-to-value factors. This aeroplane is flown to a remote strip without a flight plan and is loaded with the drugs. The flight will take-off at maximum weight of fuel and head for the USA. Since Colombia has a coastline on two oceans, the options for entry to the USA are wide. The most favoured way seems to be via the Caribbean; sometimes the flight will stop off on one of the small islands before making a run for the US coast. The cargo may be dropped at sea to a waiting boat with the aircraft heading back to South America. The runs into the USA are very hazardous as the United States Coast Guard are operating on what is a full war footing with airborne early-warning radar-equipped

Crime does not pay! Impounded drug runners at Medellin airport.

aircraft monitoring the area. When an unidentified aircraft is spotted, various different types of aircraft may be scrambled to intercept and follow it to its destination. The Coast Guard, working with local police in Florida, will try to have an armed party to greet the arrival of the drug runner. The runner is usually trying to make it to a quiet or disused airfield. In more than one case a long stretch of road has been used to land and meet accomplices to move the cargo by road to the large cities of the USA. The aeroplane may simply be left at that site, as even if they had to pay for it the profits of one successful run will more than cover its losses.

If, say, a Curtiss C-46 Commando is left, the local sheriffs department will impound it. After the due process of law it will be disposed of. Some drug runners use high-value aircraft and may join the fleet of government organisations or police forces; if they are old, like the C-46 Commando, they will be sold at auction. The person who buys it may well be the front for a drug cartel, and thus the aircraft flies south to begin its criminal career again. Not many aircraft survive many runs as the hazards are very high. These include poorly maintained aircraft, landing strips with no facilities, taking off from these whilst over-loaded, air crew who are not type-rated for the aircraft they are flying, bad weather and the risk of crashing into the sea flying low to avoid radars. Despite all this the trade continues and people still risk their lives to smuggle the drugs into the cities so that they can help to kill more people there.

Colombia's most active propliner town is that of Villavicencio. This town is the last place before the jungle and has very few roads to it, so to go anywhere you fly in or out. Some twenty different flying operators are based here and more fly in. The one sound not heard here is that of the jet engine. One or two operators use turboprops but most are piston engines.

To be found on the ramp here are up to four Curtiss C-46 Commandos, a couple of Douglas DC-4/C-54 Skymasters and the amazing number of fifteen Douglas DC-3/C-47 Dakotas from ten different operators. Some carry cargo, others only passengers, yet more will put in some seats and use the rest of the space for cargo. Locations such as

Villavicencio host a number of smaller prop types, especially as the local jungle strips are not long enough for types such as the C-46 or C-47. The de Havilland (Canada) DH(C)2 Beaver can be found. Its short take-off and landing performance plus its simple rugged construction with the ability to uplift a useful load make it a natural type for the area. Other workhorses to be found here include the twin-engined Beech 18 and the Britten-Norman BN-2 Islander.

The rest of this large continent has a mixture of old and new. The richer countries such as Brazil, which has its own aviation manufacturing industry, have jets on most routes and a better infrastructure of roads and railways which are able to move cargo. Brazil also has the Amazon which enables ocean-going ships to penetrate its heartland. The sound of the pounding piston engine is not at all common in Brazil. The same applies to Argentina, Peru, Uruguay and Chile.

Oil-rich Venezuela still manages a number of propliner operators. One of the reasons for this is its northern location, making trade easier for the islands of the Caribbean. Airports such as Ciudad Bolivar, home of Rutaca, will play host to up to ten Douglas DC-3 Dakotas, some in pristine condition and others being reduced to spares. At the capital's airport Caracas-Simon Bolivar, the sight and sound of a Douglas DC-6 from Miami or a Caribbean island will break up the noise of jets as they growl out to sea. Caracas airport is on the coast and one runway runs off to the water's edge. Propliners using this do not have to worry about any noise regulations, neither do they have to climb quickly to avoid hills or buildings. They can just take off and slowly climb to a cruise altitude with no problems.

The prop scene in South America is usually feast or famine. In some countries they are the normal means of air transport and in others they are the exception rather than the rule. They will slowly die out as the supply of airframes dries up or is written off, and the cost of AVGAS fuel becomes too expensive or the supply too scarce. It will be a sad day when South America with all its faults has no more propliners flying. It will probably be the last place on Earth where they will fly from.

A room with a view. The café window at
Villavicencio overlooks the apron and the
sight of three C-46 Commandos.

ABOVE:
C-46 HK400 of Aerosol underway at Villavicencio, its two P & W R2800 engines pounding along.

LEFT:
In the thin air of La Paz, Bolivia Universal C-46 CP746 gets ready for its next load of meat to be brought from the lowland farms to the city.

This C-46 at La Paz is under maintenance to fly. Note the lack of hangar and workshop associated with this task! What you see is what you get.

BELOW:
Cochabamba is the home of this general cargo C-46 CP1616 of North-East Bolivian Airways.

Super smart on the outside and with a full executive interior this Serca Convair 580 HK3666 flies charters around Colombia. Pictured at Medellin.

With a background of the snow-covered
Andes, this Convair 340 of CAT awaits a
propeller at La Paz.

LEFT:
Not all piston planes are fit for the scrap heap. Cochabamba is home to LAC who operate this immaculate Convair 340 CP2236.

BELOW:
Polish-built, this PZL An-2 now flies for Rutaca from its base at Ciudad Bolivar in Venezuela.

La Paz-based operator La Cumbre has a fleet of two DC-6s. Neither was airworthy.

New equipment can be found in Colombia. Aces ATR 42 HK3684X seen on a scheduled flight at Medellin.

ABOVE:
The humid jungle atmosphere of Villavicencio plays havoc with the condition of this DC-4 HK1806P.

RIGHT:
South America's own commuter. The Brazilian-built Bandeirante, operated by Aires of Colombia, HK2741, seen at Villavicencio.

Beavers can be found at any location where there is a lack of roads or good airports. HK189 of Tari at Villavicencio.

Lockheed Electra N668F *Spirit of America*
seen here at Tucson now flies cargo in
England for Hunting Cargo.

CARGO OPERATIONS

In the field of cargo operations the workhorse prop can still be found at many locations all over the world.

In the United Kingdom, Coventry-based Air Atlantique fly a pair of Douglas DC-6 cargo planes on ad hoc charters around Europe. One of the most commonly flown trips is that of car parts to the motor car industry. With industry becoming more global the large multi-national companies split their part production across several countries for cost purposes. Most transfer of parts is routine and planned and accomplished by road; however, it is not infrequent for a blip to occur in the system when parts to keep a production line running are needed in another country very quickly. The only way out of this problem is to fly the parts from the production factory to the assembly line in question. The extra cost involved is still cheaper than having a production line stop for a day or more. These big four-engine DC-6s also fly newspapers around the country at night, and especially to Northern Ireland and the Isle of Man. The alternative mode of transport, the ferry boat, would not have time to get late editions on people's breakfast tables first thing the following morning.

These aircraft can be found flying in many of the remote parts of the world as well as some of the more populous. A trip to Miami in Florida will reveal several different operators all plying their trade around the Caribbean and the northern parts of South America. The type of cargoes vary from high-value items such as racehorses and polo ponies to low-value bulk items such as toilet rolls. The basic rule is, if it is needed and it will fit in the door of the aircraft, it will be carried.

The DC-6 variants flying today are usually ex-US Air Force civilianised C-118 Lift Masters which have a large freight door and a heavy-duty floor to take the weight of the cargo. Some airliners were converted at the end of their passenger careers, but in recent years a DC-6 without a freight door or floor has not been worth a great deal. Two aircraft had the cargo loading problem eased by the fitting of a swing tail. This modification was done by the engineering department of the Belgian airline Sabena. One served in Spain with Spantax and the other in Finland with Kar-Air. Both have since crossed the Atlantic, and are operated by Northernair Cargo of Alaska, which operates the largest fleet of DC-6s in the world with a total of fifteen on the books.

To gain first-hand knowledge of what a cargo flight is like this writer decided to join a flight to see what happened. But what type to fly in, and where? The Curtiss C-46 Commando is the tramp steamer of cargo planes. They are to the European a rare aeroplane as there are no examples to be found in the whole of the continent, not even in a museum. So it has to be off to the Americas to find one. There are the meat freighters of La Paz in Bolivia and, having seen the state in which they fly, you have to be more than keen to want to travel with them. There are the general cargo flights around the Caribbean calling at Miami and Puerto Rico from bases in the Dominican Republic, but in dwindling numbers, and, again, what state do they fly in? There is Alaska, but that is a long way to travel, so who has a fleet of C-46 Commandos in the North American mainland flying under a decent airworthiness certification? The answer can be found in Winnipeg, Canada. Air Manitoba has operated a fleet of six; this has been in recent years cut down by half. One was damaged beyond repair at Pickle Lake, Ontario in a landing accident. (This C-46 C-GTPO lay stripped of recoverable parts at this remote location for several years. The value of the C-46 as a workhorse has proved so great it has since been made airworthy again by another operator.) Two more after minor accidents are out to grass at Winnipeg, so that leaves just three and they are technically up for sale.

How do you get a ride in a cargo flight? Well, ask. 'No problem,' was the answer, 'but you may have to help in moving the cargo at the other end.'

So early one fine June morning I checked into the crew room at Air Manitoba's Winnipeg head office to meet the crew for the flight that morning. The captain was Bill Bullen with Harvey McKinnon in the right-hand seat as co-pilot. Looking after the cargo as load master was another co-pilot, Dave Jackson. The route for the day was from Winnipeg (YWG, the international code for the airport) to Oxford House (YOH), drop over half the cargo and then on to Sainte Therese Point (YST) to drop off the rest of the cargo, and back to base at Winnipeg. For this trip a fuel load of 5,050lb was required, which includes reserves for diversions or other unforeseen circumstances. The C-46 burns approximately 1,000lb of fuel per hour at an operator's cost of 850 Canadian dollars per hour. On the first leg, Winnipeg to Oxford House, a fuel burn of 2,100lb at a ground speed of 151 knots was predicted; leg two, Oxford House to Sainte Therese Point, 500lb at a ground speed of 183 knots (we were a lot lighter at this point having unloaded half the cargo and burnt off half the fuel, lastly the final leg home, Sainte Therese Point to Winnipeg, 1,500lb again at a ground speed of 183 knots.

Captain Bullen, the chief pilot with Air Manitoba, announced that he was going 'to kick some tyres' and do the external inspection walk around, and he invited me to climb aboard. Walking up to the C-46 C-GTXW *Ancient Lady* you realise how much bigger the Commando is than the C-47 Dakota. I climbed the ladder which stopped a few feet short of the door to the cockpit, and a hanging rope was grabbed which is used to haul oneself into the front office. This was a true 'glass' cockpit, except all this glass is for looking out of. I took my seat behind the co-pilot and looked about. Three plates took my attention; one was its conversion to US civil status: 'N4803J c/n 30386 20/4/84 F.A. Conner Miami Aeroplane spec. 342'. (This particular aircraft, after service with the US Army Air Force, had been sold to the Government of India and then sold on to Venezuela. Later it was to be seen derelict at Miami in 1964; F.A. Conner rebuilt it in 1966 and it headed off south to Panama and then to the Dominican Republic.) The second plate was the drill to be followed in case of fire; instruction number seven in this was 'Land as soon as possible'. Personally I would have moved this up a few slots! The third plate stated 'No aerobatic manoeuvres including spins are approved'. Well, I would go along with that.

At 0740 the engines were started and at 0746 we began to taxi to runway 31. The noise during take-off is so loud it is almost painful; headsets have to be, and were, worn all the time. So loud is it that even R/T is not used on take-off; the co-pilot signals the decision speeds and take-off speeds V1 and V2 by holding up the number of fingers. At 0755 the wheels left the ground and a course of 005° North was set climbing to an altitude of 7,000 feet. This took some time to reach as the climb was very slow. The gross take-off weight today was 47,864lb and the maximum for this type is 48,000lb. The leg to Oxford House was 359 miles and took two hours nine minutes. During the flight after the coffee there was entertainment for the crew as they watched in some amusement at their passengers' attempts to fly the Commando in a straight line and at a level altitude. The aircraft does not have an auto-pilot; in fact none of the airline's fleet of DC-3 Dakotas and Hawker Siddeley HS748s have them either.

With the descent into Oxford House coming up, Captain Bill Bullen resumed control and made it look so easy. But then that is the mark of a true professional. Oxford House is a 3,500-foot strip on an Indian reservation. The elevation is 672 feet above sea level and it has few facilities, comprising a hut which acted as an all-purpose building. The approach was purely visible with no air traffic control. The landing was at eighty knots and we were soon rolling up to the 'terminal'. The crew after shutdown of the engines exited the cockpit through the door into the fuselage. I followed a few minutes later. Upon opening the door I was faced with a wall of solid cargo; the way to the back of the aircraft was to crawl along the top of this until the rear door was reached. No passageway was provided as it took up valuable space that could be used for cargo.

A pick-up truck had backed up to the cargo door and the flight crew were hard at work off-loading an assortment of items from frozen hamburgers to outboard motors to mattresses with anything in between. This flight crew were not in smart corporate uniforms but in hard work overalls and big boots; they were not afraid to get their hands dirty. The locals from the reservation for whom all this cargo was intended were in the truck loading it quickly. I did not know what to expect from the people of an Indian reservation but I did not expect to see 'heavy metal' T-shirts and jeans. Perhaps I had seen too many western films as a small boy. Captain Bill Bullen excused the passenger from the task of loading so I was able to have a wander around the area. The 'town' is a collection of small wooden huts with limited road access. The runway is a gravel strip and would make a mess of a jet engine with all those bits of loose gravel flying around.

The off-load of cargo was 7,200lb and about half the fuselage was now empty. The cargo for the next leg was still against the cockpit door, so another climb over the stacks and back into the cockpit had to be undertaken. With everyone in place the engines were started and we turned to taxi up the runway to take off. They do not have a parallel taxiway. We left Oxford House on runway 22 forty-nine minutes after landing. They do not waste time on trips like this.

The next sector was one of eighty miles and took twenty-six minutes. Sainte Therese Point is another gravel strip of 3,400 feet with 100 feet over-run. This is useful as the strip starts and finishes at the water's edge. On a cloudy day in dull light it was difficult for me to see the actual line of the runway but the crew had been there many times and we were soon rolling down the runway to off-load some 6,000lb of assorted cargo. The setting here was very similar to Oxford House, but the runway surface was far more rutted and muddy. Sainte Therese Point gets two scheduled passenger services with Perimeter Airlines Metros and Air Manitoba HS748s, both from Winnipeg.

Landing at Miami, Honduran Electra HR-TNT of TAN Carga.

Soon the aircraft was empty of cargo. The local Indians or Native Americans had got quite excited about a cargo of lumber/wood they were convinced we should have had on board for them but did not. It in fact was flown in later that day on another C-46 trip.

The time spent on the ground here was just half an hour. The take-off and flight back on this final section of the journey to Winnipeg was under the control of co-pilot Harvey McKinnon. We had taken off with a weight of 32,400lb for this 292-mile sector. This leg was to be a flight time of ninety minutes, and since the aircraft was empty of cargo and most of the fuel had burnt off an altitude of 10,600 feet was used with an airspeed of 169 knots. It was a novel sensation to see that as we flew through a cloud, rain would come into the cockpit from the co-pilot's window. As there is no positive air traffic control in the region a frequency of 122.80 VHF was used to Island Lake as an advisory channel.

Fifteen minutes and fifty miles out of Winnipeg the descent was started with a gentle 300 feet/minute rate of descent, increasing as we headed for Winnipeg's runway 36 to land. At a speed of eighty knots the main wheels touched down. During the taxi to the Air Manitoba hangar, Captain Bill Bullen took over the controls as there was a strong crosswind and the C-46 is not an easy aeroplane to control under such conditions. It has to use bursts of engine power to move it around the taxiways. Under company rules, if a Commando has to land on one engine it would have to be towed back to the hangar, as a single-engine taxi is not approved.

At 1321 hours the two Pratt & Whitney R2800 radial piston engines of 2,000 horsepower were switched off and a silence fell over the flight deck. The crew quickly got all their belongings together and we all trooped down the fuselage and out of the cargo door. The day's work for this 1942-built aeroplane was not yet over. It would be loaded up again and if all went well would be off again later that afternoon. For me my day was over. After offering my thanks to the crew for their patience with this C-46 fan, for this passenger, and with my ears still ringing to the sound of the pounding pistons, it was back to the hotel for a late lunch.

In the world of aviation almost any aeroplane is capable of carrying cargo of some description. Almost every Boeing 747 Jumbo Jet will carry cargo pallets in its hold as well as a full load of passengers. Such flights are not within the scope of this text, so what aircraft workhorse props are to be found in the cargo areas of the world's airports? (A number of types such as the Douglas DC series of four-engined airliners, the DC-4/-6/-7 plus a number of other types, are also used as water bombers, the details of which can be found in that section of the text.)

The Canadian aircraft maker Canadair built the world's first purpose-designed swing-tailed cargo aircraft. The birth of such an aircraft dates back to 1957 when the Royal Canadian Air Force asked Canadair to develop a transport version of the CL-28 Argus maritime reconnaissance and anti-submarine patrol aircraft. The CL-28 Argus has been based upon the design of the Bristol Britannia without the need to pressurise the airframe, replacing turboprop engines with pistons for fuel economy at the low levels the type was flown at. Once again using the basic Britannia design the fuselage was lengthened by 12 ft 4 in, and because of the need to fly higher the fuselage was pressurised and the turboprops brought back. A new engine was fitted. The Britannia had been powered by Bristol Proteus, but the engine chosen for the new aircraft, the Cl-44, was the Rolls-Royce Tyne. Four engines of 5,730 shaft horsepower were fitted to the swing-tail version, the CL-44D-4.

The first model of the aircraft built was the CL-44-6 for the RCAF; this did not have the swing-tail but was fitted with two side-loading doors on the left-hand side, one at the front end and the other at the rear end. For service in the RCAF it was known as the CC-106 Yukon. The prototype was flown for the first time from Cartierville in November 1959. The first of the swing-tail versions was flown for the first time exactly one year later from the same location.

The first users of the CL-44D-4 were North America's leading air cargo operators, Flying Tiger, which operated twelve, Slick Airways, which operated four, and Seaboard & Western which had six. They were able to operate at far better costs than the late model piston-engined airliners that were being used for cargo operations by this time.

Late in 1970 and early in 1971 the RCAF Yukons were taken out of military service and sold on the civil market. Many went to South America, and time has taken its toll on them. Few survive in service today, most having been destroyed in accidents.

It was a similar story for the swing-tail CL-44D-4. Going on the second-hand market from the major American carriers, they were sold all over the world where operators tended to use one or two aircraft. Once again accidents have written off a number of aircraft and the CL-44 in any version is not the most common aircraft to be found in the cargo areas of the world's airports. Total production of both the CC-106 (CL-44-6) and the CL-44D-4 was just thirty-nine.

The Lockheed Constellation is to many people the most attractive of all the propliners ever built. The distinctive shaped fuselage topped off with the triple tail unit was unique. The aircraft grew from the L-049 Constellation to the heavier L-749, then to the longer L-1049 Super Constellation and to the final version, the largest in terms of wingspan and length, the L-1649 Starliner. The first variant made its maiden flight from the Lockheed Air terminal at Burbank, California in January 1943. Despite having been designed as an airliner, the onset of World War Two meant that the type would be used as a long-range troop transport for the duration of the conflict.

The Constellation entered service with the commercial world at the end of 1945, with both Pan American and Trans World Airways. This latter company is the one most identified with the whole family of Constellations. In the first decade after the end of the war in 1945 the two large commercial aircraft manufacturers in California, Douglas and Lockheed, were head to head in a battle for sales and technical supremacy. The three Douglas DC designs, the DC-4/-6/-7, could be compared to the developments of the Lockheed variants L-049/L-749/L-1049/L-1649. In the area of technical innovations Lockheed were in the lead, but in the area of sales Douglas were well ahead on both civil and military sales figures. By the time the finest of the Lockheed designs flew for the first time in October 1956, the L-1649 Starliner had new technology looming up on it. The Starliner entered service with TWA on the London-New York service in June 1957; only one year later the jet-powered Boeing 707 and the de Havilland Comet 4 were to make the piston engine obsolete by offering the flying public a smooth and fast service. This clash with new technology led to only forty-four L-1649 Starliners being built. They mostly served on the less popular routes served by the airliners. The total build of all versions of the Constellation was 856 over sixteen years from 1943 to 1959.

When an aeroplane is not suitable for passenger service the price of the airframe will drop and the air cargo operator will move in and pick up a bargain. So it was with the Constellation. The type has served with every class of cargo operator from the large scheduled operator to the out and out crook flying contraband or drugs. They have flown to all parts of the world and at times have been abandoned there.

As the first line operators sold on their Constellations, for many operators their troubles began. The Constellation, as has been stated, was the most technically advanced piston-engined transport of its day. This technology required good maintenance, especially with the engines. As the aircraft were being operated by smaller companies who had not got the maintenance facilities of the larger carriers, things began to go wrong. The engines that powered the Constellation had got more powerful according to the development of each model: the L-049 was powered by four 2,200-hp Wright Double Cyclone R3350 radial air-cooled piston engines; the L-749 with four 2,500hp Wright 749Cs; the L-1049 Super Constellation with four 2,700hp Wright 956 Double Cyclones. A version of the Super Constellation, the L-1049C, was the first certified airliner to use a turbo-compound engine. In one of these, extra power is provided by the heat from the exhaust gases being re-used. The engine power for this variant shot up from 2,500hp for the basic L-1049 to 3,250hp with the Wright 872. The top of the range L-1649 Starliner was powered by four 3,400hp Wright R988 Turbo Cyclones.

The turbo-compound engine was in its day a very complicated piece of equipment to keep in first-class condition. Engine shutdowns were quite common even amongst the best maintained operators such as Lufthansa, not an airline that one ever thinks of when poor maintenance is talked about. It does not take a vivid imagination to see the problems of a cargo plane used by an operator who does not always comply with the law with regard to maintenance and the take-off weight maximum for the aircraft. More than one Constellation has come to grief by losing an engine when the aircraft was overweight.

The ad hoc use of the Constellation ranged from the bulk of the airlift into the beleaguered state of Biafra in West Africa in the late 1960s to spray operations against various insects in North America, with every type of operation in between. Today very few Constellations still fly in commercial operations. The last stronghold of the type has been in the Dominican Republic where the airlines AMSA-Aeroliners Mundo SA and Aerochago Airlines SA are the last commercial operators. These Constellations are from the stock of United States military C-121s released from storage at AMARC, the Aerospace Maintenance and Regeneration Center at Davis-Monthan Air Force Base in Tucson, Arizona during the late 1970s and early 1980.

The search for a replacement for the Douglas DC-3 Dakotas frustrated all aircraft manufacturers, including the Douglas company itself. It was natural for the company once they had finished production of the Dakota to want to be the company who built the aircraft to replace it. The Douglas company took the decision to take the existing Dakota airframe and modernise it rather than to try to build a totally new design. To do this they obtained two second-hand Dakotas and worked upon them. The fuselage was lengthened by 3 ft 3 in to add to the seating capacity. A new larger vertical tail was added; the wingtips and those of the horizontal tail plane were squared off. The engine nacelles were re-designed to make the undercarriage totally enclosed when it was retracted. The engines fitted were two 1,475hp Wright Cyclone R1820 nine-cylinder air-cooled radial piston engines. The first flight of the DC-3S, or, as it was known, Super Dakota, took place at Clover Field on 23 June 1949. The aircraft worked far better than was expected, and offered an all-round performance gain over the DC-3.

The problem for Douglas aircraft was that the aeroplane did not sell. After a major sales tour of the type the only firm order was for three aircraft from Capital Airways. The reason for the lack of orders was not the product: the Super Dakota was all and more than was required. Stocks and prices of basic Dakotas were such that they were available as required, but the Super Dakota was expensive. The other reason for the failure was the new family of Convair Liners, faster and pressurised, coming off production lines. Most of the major airlines went for this option.

The type would have been just a footnote in a history of Douglas if it had not been for the US Navy. The prototype had been sold to the USAF who after service trials declined to buy the type, but the aircraft was passed on to the Navy. At last an order was forthcoming. This was to convert one hundred Dakotas to Super Dakotas with the new Navy designation of R4D-8 (after 1962 known as C-117). The C-117 stayed in the US Navy and the US Marine Corps service until the mid-1970s before being withdrawn and stored at AMARC. These well maintained aircraft were soon released on to the cargo market and small operators up and down the continent could be seen using them, such as Millardair of Toronto, Canada with a fleet of six.

The trio of Convair Liners, the 240/340/440, have had and are still having a long and productive life. A lot of Convairs are still in the business of carrying passengers and it will be some time yet before these aircraft give up their airline status and carry cargo.

The history of the design can be traced to the Convair model 110 which was a thirty-seat tricycle undercarriage twin-engine airliner, built and flown in 1946. Only one was built as Convair were talking to the airlines and the need

Peruvian Electra OB-M-1328 under maintenance at Tucson.

for a forty-seat aircraft was put forward. This discussion resulted in the Convair model 240, and the type first flew in March 1947 from San Diego. The aircraft was powered by two Pratt & Whitney Double Wasp R2800 engines of 2,300hp. A first for the design was that it had a pressurised fuselage. The aeroplane sold well to the airlines with 171 delivered. The biggest boost to the type was the acceptance of the design by the US Air Force: nearly four hundred were ordered as either T-29 navigation trainers or C-131 Samaritan casualty evacuation transports.

The Convair 340 was a natural development of the 240, longer by fifty-four inches in the fuselage and having a fourteen-foot wingspan increase. The same basic engine was retained but the horsepower was increased by 100 to 2,400. The prototype of the model 340 first took to the air in October 1951. The type again sold well with 311 total production, 209 to civil customers and the balance to the US military.

The last of the piston Convairs was the model 440, known as the Metropolitan. The 440 had the same dimensions as the 340, and the main changes were in the streamlining, in the greater gross weight, and the optional weather radar that gave it a slightly longer nose. The Convair 440 flew for the first time in December 1955 and production stopped just short of the double century at 199.

Had that been the end of the story the type would have faded away slowly, leaving just a small number left in remote places. The shot in the arm for the long life of the Convair came with the plan to re-engine airframes with turboprops. The first conversions were made using a British Napier Eland of 3,060shp. But the two successful conversions in terms of sales came with the fitting of the Allison 501 of 3,750shp and the Rolls-Royce Dart of 3,000shp. The Allison has been the most successful of the two and the model number 580 was allocated to these aircraft. The Rolls-Royce-powered aircraft are designated

600 for conversions of the model 240, and 640 for conversions of 340 and 440s.

As has been stated, the type is still in airline service. The ones used by cargo operators are usually small parcel operations, feeding the large hubs of the worldwide parcel operators. In Bolivia ex-US military piston-powered Convairs are finding favour as meat freighters because of their low purchase costs. One other use for the Convair is that of an executive aircraft. With a corporate interior seating twenty people as opposed to the airline fit of up to fifty, the traveller will have far more room than a corporate jet such as a Lear Jet. The speed of the turboprop over short distances of a few hundred miles is not that much slower than the pure jet. An example of the type is used by Serca Colombia, or Servicio Espacializado de Carrga Aerea, which operates a model 580 converted from a model 340 with an executive fit interior. This superb aircraft is available for charters from the base at Bogota and has seating standards second to none.

A lot of the world's tramp cargo planes are ex-military aeroplanes that were designed for the shorter range tactical role. Two aircraft that were designed for the long-haul heavy strategic role can be found in two very different parts of the world. First the Douglas C-133 Cargomaster. The design for this transport aeroplane was started early in 1953 and the first aircraft was rolled out some three years later. It was of conventional appearance with a high wing and access being gained by a built-in rear loading ramp together with a cargo door on the port side near the front. Power was provided by four Pratt & Whitney T34 turboprops of 5,700shp, later increased to 7,500shp. The Cargomaster made its maiden flight in April 1956 and deliveries to the US Air Force began in August of the following year. The type remained in US service until 1971 when due to fatigue problems they were withdrawn to storage in Arizona at Davis-Monthan Air Force Base.

During 1973 the Foundation for Airborne Relief, a non-profit-making organisation, purchased four aircraft to carry supplies to disasters anywhere in the world. The Federal Aviation Administration, however, took a very dim view of these plans because of the type's fatigue problems, refused type certification for the project and so the idea was scrapped. By the end of the 1970s one of the Cargomasters was at Long Beach and the two others were parked up at Mojave, California.

One carrier has been successful in the operation of the C-133 and that is the aptly named Cargomaster Corporation based at Anchorage in Alaska, who have two aircraft. They are not allowed to operate general charter work and can only carry goods for either the State of Alaska Government or for the US Federal Government. They are tasked with the carriage of heavy and bulky items such as snow ploughs that could not fit into any other type.

The C-133 has a load capacity of up to 110,000lb (49,800 kg) weight and was able to carry such items as a complete ballistic missile, such as an Atlas or a Thor. The use of the aircraft is very low and they can sit for many months on end without having to perform a single cargo operation.

The British equivalent of the Cargomaster was the Short SC5 Belfast. The aircraft was produced nearly a decade later, flying for the first time in January 1964 from the manufacturer's base at Belfast. The first production aircraft joined No.53 Squadron of the Royal Air Force exactly two years after the maiden flight. For the next ten years the type operated all around the world, carrying heavy and bulky loads for the British military. The defence cuts in the mid-1970s had the Belfast phased out of service, leaving the RAF without a heavy freighter for many years until the Lockheed Tristar was purchased. The total production of the Belfast was just ten aircraft. One was preserved and most of the others were scrapped for their engines. Three aircraft, however, found a home with Heavy Lift Cargo Airlines of Stansted in Essex. The company specialises in the carriage of heavy and bulky items of cargo. For this the Belfast is perfect. The hold in the fuselage is ninety feet long, thirteen feet high and sixteen feet wide; added to this is a capacity to lift 85,000lb (38,556 kg). Small wonder that when a high-value cargo needs to be moved quickly, Heavy Lift are the first to be called. The sort of job that they have been called upon to carry out was the delivery of three Westland Lynx helicopters for the Nigerian Republic Navy. All three fitted in one aeroplane. The SC5 Belfast is powered by four Rolls-Royce Tyne turboprops of 5,730shp each.

The most bizarre cargo aircraft flying today has to be the Guppy. The need for an aeroplane to carry large bulky sections of spacecraft from the manufacturers in California to the Cape Canaveral (Kennedy) Space Center in Florida became apparent in the early 1960s. The parts were too big to go by road or rail, and a sea journey took far too long, was costly and carried the risk of salt-water damage to delicate rocket parts. The answer was to convert an existing aircraft, in this case a Boeing 377 Stratocruiser. The job was undertaken by Aerospace Lines at Van Nuys, California. The Stratocruiser was chosen for two reasons: one, they were unwanted by airlines so the cost was low; and two,

they were large, powerful aircraft. The conversion required two aircraft. The one being converted had a sixteen-foot section of fuselage from the spare aeroplane spliced into the airframe. The cabin was built on the outside giving a bulbous result. The name of Guppy came when one person said it looked like a 'pregnant guppy'. The name stuck and the initials PG were added to the type designation, Boeing 377PG. The Guppy was able to carry sections of spacecraft up to 34,000lb (15,422 kg) in weight.

The type was a success and two versions were built. One was the Mini Guppy. This featured a swing-tail for loading and, like the original 'Pregnant Guppy', was powered by the original Stratocruiser engines, four Pratt & Whitney R4360 Double Wasp air-cooled radial piston engines of 3,500hp each. The second variant was the model 201 Super Guppy, and this was powered by turboprops. These engines were taken from surplus US Navy Lockheed P-3 Orions and were Allison AN501s of 4,500shp each. The access for cargo in the Super Guppy was provided by the entire nose section of the aircraft swinging open to port.

Today there are two users of Guppys. One is Erickson Air Crane Company of Central Point, Oregon which operates a Mini Guppy. This aircraft was formerly operated by Aero Union, the water bomber conversion company, as an outsize cargo aircraft from its base at Chico, California until the late 1980s. The major Guppy user today is Airbus Industries of Toulouse in southern France. Airbus is one of the major players in the world of building airliners. It is a multi-national company with parts being built in Spain, Germany and the United Kingdom. All the parts need to be transported to the assembly lines at Toulouse and many parts are too big to be sent a long way by road. The wings are the perfect example of this. The manufacture of all the wings for all the different versions of the airbus takes place at the British Aerospace Plant at Broughton near Chester in North Wales. When a set of wings is complete they are loaded on a low loader vehicle and taken to Manchester International Airport, a distance of about forty miles. When they arrive a Super Guppy is scheduled to be there to collect the wings and fly them to the south of France. Airbus use four aircraft and they are kept very busy flying components around the skies of Europe. So busy are they that Airbus is planning to convert up to four Airbus A300 jets to a Guppy-like configuration over the next five years. Some people may find it ironic that Airbus could not function without the aid of what were once Boeing airliners, Boeing, of course, being the major competitor to Airbus in the world's new airliner market.

In the United Kingdom a type that has been hitherto almost unseen with British airlines has started to operate in growing numbers. This is the Lockheed L-188 Electra. The aeroplane dates from December 1957 when it first flew from the Lockheed Air terminal at Burbank in California. Ten months later the first airline deliveries commenced to Eastern Airlines. In front-line airline service the Electra had several problems to contend with. The first was a series of accidents that lost it public confidence, despite the fact that Lockheed found the problem, excess vibration that in turn led to failure of the wing root, and successfully cured it. The second was that the pure jet was entering service only

Now down to just one aircraft in service, the Vanguard had a long service as both an airliner and as a freight carrier. G-APEK of Air Bridge waits for its night cargo of newspapers at Liverpool.

a short time later, and the travelling public wanted to fly in pure jets.

The Electra went on to give sterling service in smaller airlines or as back-up types for the larger carrier. Cargo conversions were a natural development and the Lockheed Aircraft Service Company themselves converted forty aircraft by fitting reinforced floors and cargo doors. Many more aircraft were converted by other operators.

In the late 1980s Air Bridge, based in the East Midlands at Castle Donnington, began to introduce the Electra to its fleet of ageing Vickers Vanguards. This cargo airline, now renamed Hunting Cargo Airline, has all but changed its fleet around. In 1990 the fleet was three Electras and seven Vanguards. By 1993 the situation had changed to eight Electras and just three Vanguards. With a higher build figure, 170 being constructed, and sharing the same basic engine, the Allison AN501/T56 turboprop of 3,750shp, with both the Lockheed P-3 Orion (this type is a direct development of the Electra) and the Lockheed C-130 Hercules, the spares problems for operating Electras are a great deal fewer than for the Vickers Vanguards which had a production run of just forty-four including the first prototype.

The Vanguard was designed by Vickers as a follow-on to the successful Viscount. The first flight was in January 1959. Only two airlines, BEA – British European Airways (now part of British Airways) – and TCA – Trans Canada Airlines (now Air Canada), purchased the type before production was stopped. The reason for the lack of sales success is similar to the Lockheed Electra: it came out at a time when jets were beginning to appear, and the public view of any aeroplane with propellers was that it must be old, even if it was the latest state-of-the-art turboprop airliner powered by a new Rolls-Royce engine, the Tyne, with a power output of 4,980shp. The economics of running a Vanguard were excellent, but by the late 1960s Air Canada was taking the type out of service, and during the same time-frame BEA was doing the same.

A cargo conversion was the obvious thing to do with what was still a very good, efficient and economic aircraft. Aviation Traders at Southend did the first conversion in 1969 and supplied the kits for BEA to convert another seven at their home base at Heathrow. The new conversions had heavy-duty floors, loading systems and a large port-side freight door at the forward end of the fuselage. A new name was given to the new role, Merchantman. Over the years the number of aircraft has dwindled to just three in service, and they may not last for long before they are retired and scrapped.

It would seem to be the fate of many aircraft designs that have reached the end of their passenger days, either through sheer age or lack of appeal, to carve themselves a new role in life as a cargo plane. Long may the world's airports resound to the growl of pounding piston or the high-pitched whine of the turboprop. These workhorses will fly on long into the next century.

RIGHT:
Britain's premier prop operator Air Atlantique operates two DC-6s. G-SIXC is seen at its Coventry base.

BELOW:
DC-6 N84BL of Aerial Transit taxis into Miami after a Caribbean cargo run.

With all P & W R2800 engines turning, Colombian DC-6 HK1276W arrives at Bogota.

RIGHT:
Willow Run in Detroit is home to motor industry freight movements. Zantop Airlines DC-6 N4061K waits for its car part cargo.

BELOW:
Trado of the Dominican Republic operates this DC-6 HI454CT from the capital Santo Domingo.

Fancy colour schemes cost money, so many cargo operators keep aircraft in bare metal. DC-6 N28CA lands at Miami.

Air Colombia Dakota HK3292 departs
Bogota with parts for the oil industry.

BELOW:
Bogota-based Interandes operates a
number of executive aircraft together with
this Dakota HK1149.

Dakota N23SA was converted by Conroy with three P & W Canada PT6s. It is seen here in Polair colours at Bakersfield CA.

ABOVE:
The dry Arizona desert is ideal for storage without corrosion. Convairs line up at Marana for future jobs.

RIGHT:
Convair 340 N14CD still carries the livery of its European past in the colours of Scanbee. Seen here at Fort Lauderdale FL.

LEFT:
San Juan in Puerto Rico is home to many workhorse props. Honduran-operated DC-7 HR-ALY taxis to take-off.

BELOW:
Aerochago L-1049 Constellation HI 548CT lands at Miami on its regular cargo flight from Dominica. It shows the classic lines of Lockheed's finest propliner.

A general view across the ramp at Santo
Domingo in the Dominican Republic.

Three Constellations can be seen in this view of Santo Domingo's ramp. As many as will be seen anywhere.

Miami plays host to Canadair CL-44 HC-BHS of AECA Ecuador.

BELOW:
Canadair CL-44 N908L of CAX waits at Sanford FL for its next load.

Tradewinds CL-44 N106BB with its swing-tail open unloads its cargo at Santo Domingo.

BELOW:
Mojave in California is the last resting
place for these Douglas C-133 Cargomasters.

OPPOSITE:
Aerochago of Dominica operated this
Boeing C-97, seen at a very wet Miami.

Piston-powered Mini Guppy N422AU of
Aero Union seen at its Chico CA home.

Turboprop-powered Super Guppy F-BTGV
of Airbus Industries lands at Manchester to
collect another set of British-built Airbus
wings.

Aviation Traders' ATL98 Carvairs still operating can be counted on one hand. Academy Airlines N83FA gets engine maintenance at Griffin GA.

ABOVE:
Against a background of Miami's terminal, Skycharter Cargo Beech 18 N64819 plies its trade.

RIGHT:
Pickle Lake, Ontario was to have been the last resting place of Air Manitoba's C-46 C-GTPO after a landing accident. Such is the worth of the Commando it was sold and rebuilt by a new operator.

Departing Miami's Runway 27L, Rich Industries C-46 N5370N with a load of cargo. The airline has disposed of its cargo aircraft and now just operates passenger charters.

ABOVE:
Winnipeg in Manitoba was Canada's Commando capital. C-GIBX is seen on the ramp.

RIGHT:
The P & W R2800 piston engine of this Air Manitoba C-46 receives attention before its next flight.

Air Manitoba Commando C-GTXW taxis in at Winnipeg from a cargo flight up-country to Indian reservations.

OPPOSITE:
The wonderful artwork on the tail of C-46
C-GTXW *Ancient Lady*.

BELOW:
A C-46's P & W R2800 engine pounding
away on a flight from Winnipeg to Oxford
House with an assortment of cargo.

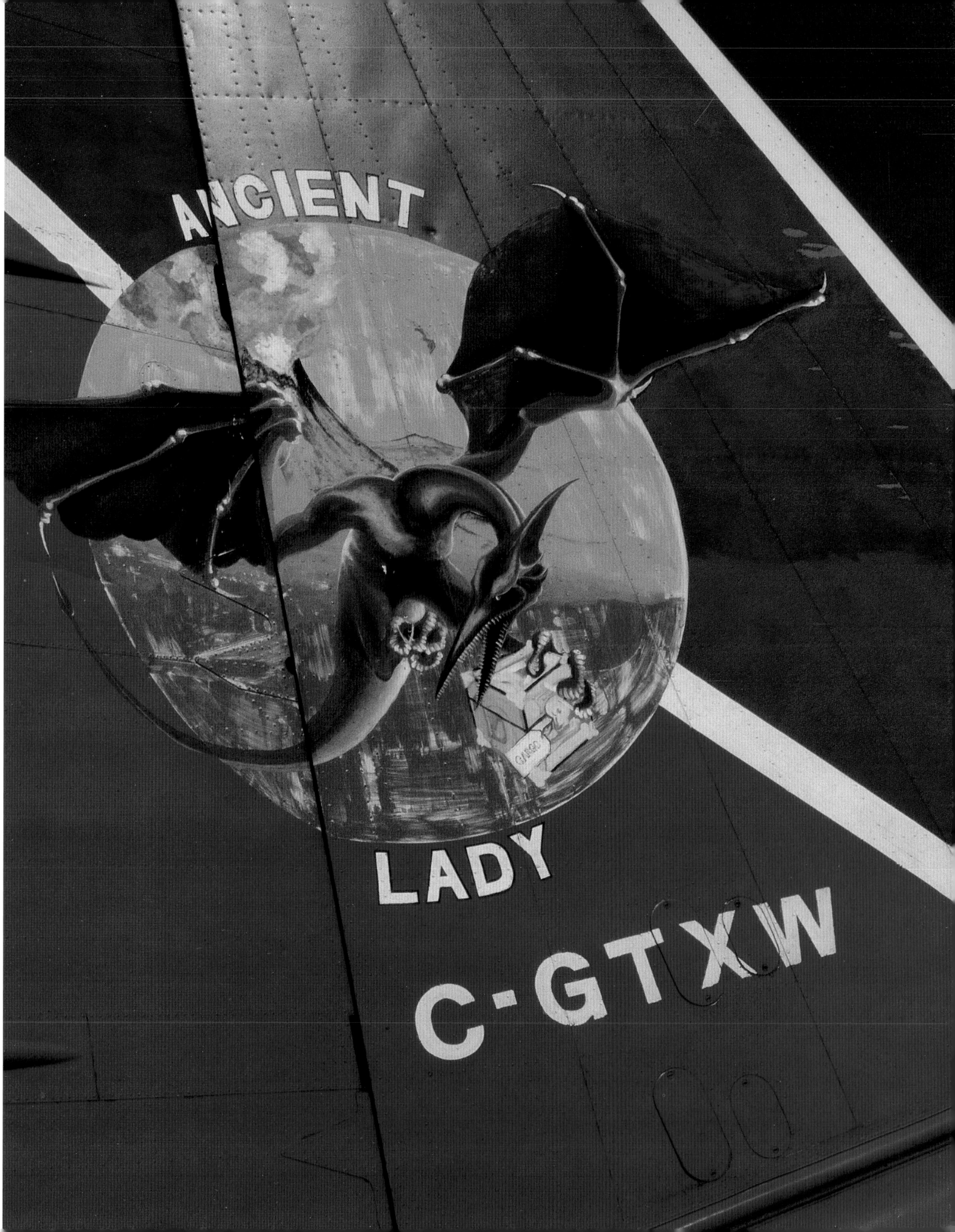
ANCIENT
LADY
C-GTXW

RIGHT:
Toronto-based Millardair had to cease trading because of available airport slots. In happier times C-54 Skymaster C-GDWZ at home base.

BELOW:
What must be the smartest Skymaster flying. Contract Air Cargo's N4989K at Borinquen in Puerto Rico.

Tall tail C-117 Super Daks are slowly finding their way on to the market. N212DD is worked on at Opa Locka FL.

RIGHT:
Scottish Aviation-built, this rugged 'go anywhere' STOL transport, G-AZHJ, is seen at Staverton.

BELOW:
The RAF kept Varsity T1 WL679 in service with the RAE at Farnborough for many years after the type's retirement from general service. It is seen landing at Fairford for an air show.

In the Cascade mountains of Washington state Piper Pawnee N7340Z is parked awaiting the next crop to spray at Wenatchee-Fancher.

Operating mixed passenger and cargo
flights, this Perimeter Airlines Metro
C-FHOZ loads up at Winnipeg.

BIBLIOGRAPHY

Alexander, Jean — *Russian Aircraft since 1940,* Putnam & Co, London, 1975

Andrews, C.F. & Morgan, E.B. — *Vickers Aircraft since 1908,* Putnam & Co, London, 1988

Barnes, C.H. — *Shorts Aircraft since 1900,* Putnam & Co, London, 1989

Bowers, Peter M. — *Boeing Aircraft since 1916,* Putnam & Co, London, 1989;

Curtiss Aircraft 1907-1947, Putnam & Co, London, 1979

Francillon, René J. — *Grumman Aircraft since 1929,* Putnam & Co, London, 1989;

Lockheed Aircraft since 1913, Putnam & Co, London, 1982;

McDonnell Douglas Aircraft since 1920, Putnam & Co, London, 1979

Gradidge, J.M.G. — *The Douglas DC-3 and its Predecessors,* Air Britain, 1984

Klee, Ulrich — *JP Airline Fleets,* Bucher & Co, Zürich, various editions

Molson, K.M. & Taylor, H.A. — *Canadian Aircraft since 1909,* Putnam & Co, London, 1982

Swanborough, Gordon Bowers, Peter M. — *United States Military Aircraft since 1909,* Putnam & Co, London, 1989;

United States Naval Aircraft since 1911, Putnam & Co, London, 1976

Wegg, John — *General Dynamics Aircraft and their Predecessors,* Putnam & Co, London, 1990

Parked outside the terminal at Bimini,
Mallard N2442H awaits the passengers for
the short flight to Miami.